For information about permission to reproduce selections from this book,   please see
webpage www.conversationfromhell.com

For information about special discounts for bulk purchases
please contact (714)-319-4370.

ISBN 978-0-9983096-1-3

$$24 \bigtimes 6$$

THE MILLENNIALS'
CONVERSATION FROM HELL

WHY THEY SHALL BE DENIED

24 X 6

Contents

CONVERSATION FROM HELL

Today's America

The problem is nobody gets it. Well not nobody, just not the people. It's not enough to say that the system is rigged, because that would suggest that the system had merit. But the system never had merit. The system was never about us, the people, the system was always about them. They built it so that they could control us. The system is for them. The system of representative democracy has always been about them; it's always been about: us versus them. It's never been a system of liberating the masses, it's always been about controlling the masses. The representative system of government, and its brand of leadership, is their system, not ours; it's their system based on deception and betrayal, not accountability as we have been told. That's the system's true purpose, and that's been its purpose from the beginning. The truth is, it's all a lie; and worse still, it always has been.

But how was Maddi to know, the prevailing propaganda was all she knew; why, because it's all she'd ever been taught. Maddi wasn't about politics, she was about family, boyfriends and although she didn't know it, her primary concern was mostly about not disappointing her parents. Growing up in a small town Maddi was taught to believe in people, trust her elders and believe that those people who are supposed to look after people would actually do their job. Generally, she thought the world was a good place and that most people were trying to make things better. She had no idea that there is, and was, a larger alternate agenda that is, and always has been, behind our institutions of government that

1

no one was talking about. She had no idea, as is the purpose with most cons, that the illusion is set up by the illusionist so far in advance, that by the time the audience is asked to look upon the presentation being made, that they are so focused on the specific spectacle before them, that they are now blind to the very charade that is being perpetrated upon them. That is why history is so important, because it shows the tricks and agendas that have been previously pursued. Of course none of Maddi's history teachers ever told her that, but that's because those teachers probably never saw themselves as part of the political charade being played out. Why, because the charade of the past is still going on; and to describe American history generally, as a charade, is apt to appear, well... un-American; well... un-American to some.

Of course, Maddi, like everyone else, understood that there was frequent corruption everywhere, but systemic corruption or institutional corruption by design; such things were possibilities that Maddi and her friends had never really thought about. Why would they, it wasn't taught in school and although every night there were the reminders on the news, in contrast to the rest of the world, America wasn't a dictatorship, but a proven democracy, which from its inception had been founded on the principles of liberty, equality, free speech and justice for all. So how could there be systemic corruption by design, clearly such structural flaws would have been exposed and cleared up by now, right? For Maddi and her friends, corruption was a matter of specifics, recurring singular events, isolated incidents in the headlines due to corrupt individuals being personally exposed proving that bad apples could still fall from a good tree, but clearly the tree itself was fine. In fact, the very fact that these scandals were being frequently exposed, was proof itself that the system worked; maybe not perfectly, but still worked.

Individual corruption itself is in the end just another (personal) evil that has to be fought continuously from one generation to the next, on a case by case basis. Never did it occur to Maddi, or the millions of her generation, that such a self-satisfying (distracting) conclusion (away from the system) was itself, the desired and designed effect.

Now Oak Valley, New York, isn't really that small a town, it would be considered a small city in some other states, but the Oak Valley residents had fought the state legislature to keep it designated as a town by gerrymandering its suburbs so as to manipulate and reduce its total declared population. The residents it seems, just wanted to preserve and convey a small town atmosphere. Oak Valley's layout however was relatively standard, as a developing municipality is apt to be, there was the original old part of town with the cluster of colonial red brick buildings that had been preserved from the first City Hall when the town's initial population was still counted in the hundreds. Across the street, was a hundred and forty- year old pub called the Angry Horse which is said to be one of the original pubs, and where it is claimed that Theodore Roosevelt had actually stopped in once or twice. Down the street from the old City Hall, but on the same side as the Horse, is the County Court House from 1835, which is still in use but has had at least two unfortunate and awkward institutional additions, so as to spoil much of the buildings original charm. Also still standing is Oak Valley's first board and batten one room school house, with its classic iconic bell holding steeple, which has now been converted into a community center used for Veteran's meetings, Cub Scouts and the occasional sporadic local charity bingo night.

Moving out from the heritage core, Oak Valley is then progressively besieged block by block with the onset of the more typical urban sprawl, where the town's streets have been overtaken by the requisite convenience stores, strip malls and corner gas stations. But as one withdraws further to the outskirts of town, the more central commercial congestion gives way to expansive oak tree covered neighborhoods where the winding streets are shaded by the canape of the century old foliage. Here amongst manicured lawns, running sprinklers and the ageless task of children trying to discover just how far a mother's eyesight really goes; Maddi had grown up, gone to primary school, middle school and attended patriotically Oak Valley's own, Mayflower Secondary School. This was Maddi's life, and it was as wholesome as a young girl's life could be. In fact, by her parents design it was exactly what they had hoped for, all that was missing was the future prospects of a good stable job, maybe a nice boyfriend and of course ultimately, maybe, hopefully marriage and grand kids. Why not? Maddi's mom was a retired nurse and her dad was a loans officer with Citibank within a few years of retirement, ... everything was perfect right? Well, not quite.

What would turn out to be missing from this middle class American dream, would oddly enough be, Maddi's own pursuit of the American dream. Why, because as Maddi was to embark on what would become the pursuit of the rest of her life, she was about to discover that for her, and for all those of her millennial generation ... the rules had changed.

Now it should not be surprising, given Maddi's Oak Valley upbringing, that Maddi saw an allure to a bigger playground. So

4

with a young girl's genetic love for retail, and armed with unimaginable burden of future student loans firmly in hand, off she went to study marketing at City College in New York City. Now as ambitious as this may seem, Maddi's move to New York City was not without her parent's reluctant blessing, for on Maddi's mother's side Maddi had family in the city, in her mother's brother, her uncle Robert, who was a graduate from Cornell and who was a lawyer by day and a political science professor by night.

As far as lawyers go, Robert was pretty good, but when it came to juries he was exceptional. Straight out of law school, in 1989 Robert joined the Manhattan County's prosecutors' office where, because of his specialty in constitutional law he seemed to be a good fit with the senior DA, who still at the end of the 80's had a budget for hiring young new attorneys. And right from the start, Robert was a hit with pretty much everyone, in that he was extremely likeable and his likeability was probably based on two prominent characteristics. First, it was clear to everyone that Robert had an obviously damaged right arm from birth, which to the casual observer made his arm appear seized and crumpled. The other feature was that in a profession full of "ego" maniacs, Robert simply didn't have one. That's not to say that Robert wasn't immensely proud, for that wasn't the case, he was extremely proud; but rather Robert was a straight forward team player, he actually took more pride in the success of any team he was on, than in any individual successes he may have had. Now normally in the prosecutor's office, a team aspect wouldn't be something that was readily available, but because Manhattan County's caseload had increased so much throughout the eighties it was decided, for management purposes, to break the office down, into four teams. Consequently, Robert found himself, upon his hire, simply assigned to the Blue team. What made Robert stand out from the very beginning, especially in this new team regiment, was the simple fact that Robert didn't try to unload his cases on to anyone else. In fact, as the years went by the opposite became true, because as the office continued to grow and pick up additional new recruits, Robert's reputation seemed to grow as he could be counted on by rookie prosecutors to step in on their behalf and personally authorize some of the more controversial plea deals. In order to protect the recruits Robert would place those deals under his name, so that if there was ever a public or media backlash it would be on Robert, and not the rookie, who took the hit.

After his day job, Robert filled his evenings as being a part time lecturer in political science and business law at NYU. He could do this because either due to his arm, or simply because he was somewhat odd looking, Robert was forever a bachelor. He was able to teach both basic business law and political science because his formal education in constitutional law made him well suited for political science, but when it came to teaching freshman the basics in business law, that opportunity came to him because in one particular year there was an opening due to a sudden illness, so Robert took it, and since the students seemed to take to him, the Dean of the Commerce Dept., simply chose to keep him on. Although Robert was proud to be a student favorite; years later, was disheartened (with respect to the web site "Rate Your Professor") to discover that in the category of "sex appeal" he had routinely received, year after year, the solid score of zero.

Sex appeal and physical deformity aside however, the requirements of these two professions did seem to work in tandem to contribute to Robert's immense success in both arenas of the courtroom and the classroom combined. Because it was in being the best teacher possible that Robert was able to become a skilled advocate, and it was in being a skilled advocate that Robert learned to perfect the fine art of teaching. So in both jobs, especially in jury settings, what made Robert successful was that he learned the power of persuasion by perfecting the craft of storytelling. In fact, in his political science course Robert would start his introductory lecture by writing on the front board the following formula of: $K + I = P = P$ and asking his class to decipher it. Although many of the students were able to readily formulate that "K" stood for knowledge and that "I" stood for intelligence, most wanted to presume that the first "P" stood for power, leaving the same group to ponder what the second "P" stood for. But the point that Robert wanted them to understand was that before you can acquire Power in anything, by using both the tangible attributes of knowledge and intelligence, you must first master the art of Persuasion. Only with the necessary ingredient of persuasion does one then ultimately acquire the subsequent achievement of Power. And of course what the students rarely consciously recognized however, was that the exercise itself was not so much an explanation of any proven scientific equation, but rather more an indirect or subliminal exercise in gaining each student's individual trust, because a student who feels that a teacher is actually trying to empower each one of them individually, is more likely to create a student who will actually attend class and try to learn something.

This was what made Robert so successful at what he did. Whether it be in teaching a class or trying to convince a jury, Robert naturally understood that there was almost always an agenda within an agenda, that in the world of human affairs, anything designed by humans was never as simple as it appeared. The biggest issue of all was whether the two or more agendas being pursued (hidden or not) were healthy and progressive. And when Robert would attempt to explain this to his political science students, the students would try to process this reality by comparing it to a sports analogy of looking for "a game within a game." But for Robert this analogy was deeply flawed; because in politics, to reduce the injustices of the world to an analogy of a game scenario is to trivialize (and more importantly abstract) the hardships of human suffering, in a way that generates a self- perpetuating perspective of self-interest and indifference. And if this was, and still is, the subliminal agenda that a society perpetuates most with any sports/politics analogies, then the students and the general public at large need to be on their guard that in making such superficial analogies; society itself, as a whole may have already in fact been played. So although such a sports comparison ought to be forgiven at a first glance, Robert found the routine comparison between sports and life, especially in matters of grave politics, to be part of the problem. In fact, it would be Robert's direct suggestion on this matter that any analogies that serve to trivialize or desensitize us from human suffering may itself, in a world beset with wealth disparity, be part of a larger hidden agenda.

Therefore, for Robert, as a teacher, what was absolutely critical for the students to understand was that in business, politics and life, there is an actual war being fought between good and evil; but it isn't the war that the media or our institutions or party candidates portray. Rather, it is the fight in life, within each individual to define themselves in their own way that allows each individual (and humanity itself) the ability to grow and flourish without self-destruction. The true struggle in life is not the type of struggle therefore that is best described by a typical win or lose scenario, but rather is better served and understood as a healthy struggle for evolution. And the fight between good and evil isn't the cartoonish battle where the lines are clear and sides are drawn and where final champions are declared; but rather the real struggle for human endeavor is the endless battle for the advancement of human growth as opposed to that which leads to destruction and decay, for both the individual, and collectively for all of us as a species. The concept of evil therefore is real, but it starts within each of us internally, as we strive to grow and evolve as individuals throughout our lives, so the question in the end isn't whether we won or lost, but whether we evolved each as individuals unencumbered by external manipulation or other undisclosed hidden agendas. This is the battle between good and evil, good is uninhibited evolution, evil is decay and destruction brought about by ignorance, sloth and indifference, or externally brought about through the selfish manipulation of others, for the purposes of corruption and greed. There can be no free evolution if there is a hidden plan for manipulation. And Robert understood this, that's why in making his arguments to his class he would quote Mick Jagger (to get their attention) who suggested that the people who ultimately killed the Kennedys, was well "you and me." Heavy stuff for a bunch of undergraduates, who thought they were going to school in order to get a well- paying job; but again, Robert wanted them to understand, that too, was part of the problem. In politics and in life, evil is about choices, especially artificial choices, that are actually designed to oppress through the maintenance of the status quo, and that's tough stuff to teach (any generation), but especially tough to teach from inside a classroom.

Understanding Betrayal

As an academic Robert was so angry at the world because somehow he felt that he (and probably too many others) had missed the real message. Growing up, Robert's mom was a true warrior and it was she who taught him the true meaning of courage, because in the 1960's to be an immigrant family from Birmingham, England after the war; and being a woman with only the equivalency of a high school education, having a son with an obvious deformity, put all the burden on her to champion her son's cause. Medically, it was clear that Robert's arm was underdeveloped, and it seemed equally clear that there was little that could be done to replace the growth that time had already denied. But that wasn't the worst of it. What made matters worse was that with this deformity, the doctors seemed to arrogantly question the development of Robert's entire right side; causing those same doctors to then speculate openly about the future prospects of Robert's future mental development. And of course, it being the sixties, such terms as "retardation" and "simpleton" were more casually used back then, then they are now, because they were thought to be scientific matters-of-fact, with little consequence given to the social stigma attached because those diagnosed with such things were thought to have few future prospects to begin with. The thinking back then was that such damaged individuals would themselves be immune from such social stigma, because ... well, they were too slow to understand such things anyway. Such fatalistic prognoses as these, made in the sixties primarily by male doctors (because back then there were just too few female doctors to challenge them); allowed such casual statements as these to take on a condescending sense of hopelessness with an elitist sense of authoritarian finality. But of course, Robert's mom, armed with her high school diploma, would have none of it.

Of course, Robert wasn't "a retard" and the fact that it was alternatively suggested that: "well, he will probably be a person of modest achievement, so it is best that we not hope for too much" as infuriating as such insults and condescension was; oddly enough this was not what made Robert, as an adult, truly so very mad. What did make Robert eternally angry was not the arrogant misdiagnosis in his own particular case, but rather the betrayal of trust that came from those very persons who were supposed to be looking out for him. It was their ego and their denial of what could be done, and their refusal to actually do their best, it was that betrayal that posed the greatest threat to Robert's future. It was Robert's mother who defied the experts and wouldn't allow the teachers to acquiesce to the casual medical comments put recklessly on various state reports that gave the institutions the excuses they needed to hold Robert back. It was his mom who recognized that an obvious deformity would probably be responsible for a child to become withdrawn and reclusive rather than be a true indicator of what he was actually capable of. Yet through it all, as saintly as she was, Joan refused to see this professional inadvertence as the problem; for her, Joan would not, and could not believe that people would ever knowingly betray their oath, or selfishly put their own egos or self- interest ahead of those whom they were paid to protect. It didn't make sense to Joan that for no reason at all people would simply not do their job. They were being paid, and it was they themselves who had chosen the health care profession to begin with, it was their chosen career, so they must be good people at heart, right? So naturally they must be doing their job, right? And sure everyone has a bad day, but surely they must be trying to do their best, right? So because Joan, herself was selfless, Joan couldn't see the battle taking place inside others, between what Joan understood from her upbringing to be just simple human courtesy, responsibility and decency, to do right by others; and the selfish failure by others to even do their job due to such things as apathy, laziness, or ego.

To Joan, what was happening to her and her son, was counter intuitive. She could not believe that others especially professionals, would allow their own petty selfish concerns such as their own lethargy or their personal egos, to interfere with a patient's own future best interests. Joan had just lost her father fighting Hitler, and clearly the Nazi's were evil, surely there was no comparison between what just happened in Europe and a doctor's own egotistical apathy. To Joan, such trivial concerns on a day-to-day basis were nothing more than selfish and pathetic individual failures. For Joan, having just faced down the Second World War, and since Joan herself was completely unselfish; she couldn't see how one's own personal daily frustrations with doctors, teachers and various administrative agencies, could be anything more than individual disappointments and isolated incidents. For Joan there was no larger problem (again, because she and her generation had just beat back the Nazi's) than what the world had just gone through with Word War II, so individual human failures were to her, just that, individual failures; and therefore any daily difficulties just had to be dealt with on a case-by-case basis.

What was invisible to Joan however, was that with each individual let-down, with each frustrating denial, each promise broken, a systemic societal acceptance of betrayal was being permanently forged as being "the norm." Joan, due to her own good nature and her belief in human decency generally, was therefore blind to the prospect of a societal death by a thousand cuts. Joan was a survivor and fighter, so due to her own ability to persevere, Joan was oblivious to the fact that there was a long societal rot that was deepening with each generation that was perpetuating the human acceptance of abandonment and betrayal. People were good, right? And the allies had just defeated the Nazi's and the Fascists so that kind of evil had been beaten, right? And the United Nations had just been created, so the west was good, right? Clearly, such massive struggles as these were the true struggles between good and evil, not the daily minutia of petty jealousies being played out within the consciences of specific weak individuals. For Joan, the global conflicts and atrocities that she had just survived and witnessed were clearly distinguishable from the insular squabbles of whether or not on a particular day, a particular individual, had actually done his or her job. To Joan such daily failings were just that, individual failings, that were completely disassociated from anything that could be considered systemic or fostered by society itself. For Joan, the failings of each individual were not the failings of the state but the individual failings of a particular person on a particular day. From Joan's perspective America was not, nor could it ever be, held responsible for what individuals failed or refused to do. If individuals failed their professional responsibility because of their own personal flaws or self- interests, that was their fault due to their choices. America didn't make people do what they did, clearly: its people who do what they do. American institutions are mechanisms for liberation, not destruction. Surely the U.S. Constitution couldn't be, held responsible for the pettiness of man. The U.S Constitution gave us representative democracy and the American Bill of Rights in order to free

13

ourselves, so clearly from Joan's perspective, the constitution and democracy were not to blame. According to history, we made the U.S. Constitution and all the institutions that followed it, such as the United Nations; so clearly these things were created by man, we forged them; they did not forge us, right? So if the argument is to be made that: the choices that man makes on a daily basis have in fact been hindered by our institutions; "well 'our history' will tell you, sir; that you have it backwards, and that you are indeed wrong."

Now Robert being his mother's son, he too strove to see the best in people especially from those people, who openly proclaimed through their profession, title or office, to be looking out for others. But for Robert, unlike his mother, Robert was to have an additional analytical perspective. Robert had always been fascinated with the study of history, especially constitutional history' and it was this study of history that allowed him to see certain recurring themes of struggle within society that were forever being replayed out over and over again, despite the creation of various institutions that were specifically created to alleviate and prevent such struggles. For Robert, despite his mother's upbringing to trust and see the best in people, Robert had learned from his own experiences in his youth and from his various battles as a lawyer as well, that just because something was portrayed to represent a particular ideal, that unfortunately in the history of human affairs, rarely did that representation make that ideal a reality. Rather it is more the norm that the ideal that is usually put up as the ultimate goal for an aspiring institution, is itself undermined by another competing hidden agenda (or agenda's) that operate in the subtext or shadows of the stated ideal. The institution thus becomes the front or distraction for the operation of the sub-agenda, while the supposed pursuit of the ideal within the institution preoccupies the masses with the never ending hope that the ideal and the prospects for that ideal are still possible. So for Robert, the recurring theme that appeared most repeatedly throughout history was the fight for power and control of all things, and the willingness of so many of the powerful, to avoid the hard work and to simply acquire that power and control through false promises and deception. And with this recurring theme, so began Robert's fascination with politics.

Now of course, Robert hadn't always been a successful teacher and lawyer, for he too had started as a student sitting in massive lecture halls with bolted down seats much like the students who now appeared before him; and of course he too, like them, Robert had his favorite teachers. And though most of Robert's in depth knowledge came from his university years, it was his grade seven American history teacher who got him started down his eventual path. Mr. McCoy was that teacher and the reason he had such a profound impact on Robert was because not only was he Robert's teacher at the impressionable age of thirteen, but also Mr. McCoy taught Robert that education itself, can be meaningless unless you try to give it meaning by making sense of what it is your learning. In trying to make this point, Mr. McCoy would explain that history is itself worthless, if it is just used for the board game, Trivial Pursuit. Now in a best case scenario, every student has at some point in his or her life a "Eureka" moment when for him or her the penny drops and what is being taught suddenly clicks and things just start to make sense. This is the moment when all the facts and theorems within any given subject matter or discipline, stop being just a bunch of stuff, and actually become recognizable building blocks inside the head of the student studying them. Such a moment like this is usually when the task of studying stops being the painful homework that we all associate with school, and starts to become fun, or ... at least something that is somewhat interesting. It was Mr. McCoy who provided such a moment for Robert. In Mr. McCoy's class, Robert began to see history not as a disassociated turn of archaic events, but rather as an operational thing that is best understood as a multi- dimensional continuum of human effort that visibly works towards a discernable purpose. And when it became apparent to Robert that human-history might be best understood as a purposeful thing with an actual agenda, well now that: for Robert (even at the age of 13), was "something interesting."

So as Robert was to take his search for the purpose of human history to university, Robert was to engage his studies with the benefit of two parallel perspectives. First, his initial instinct was to see people, as his mother had taught him, as individuals who were inherently good and who, themselves, wanted to be good. This was how Joan had wanted Robert and his sister Susan, Maddi's mom, to see and treat others. From this perspective, Robert understood that it ought to follow that as people supposedly go about doing their jobs, and apply their respective professions to others (whether it be to their patients, clients, congregation, constituents or what-have-you) that these representatives ought to be presumed to be trying to do the right thing. This was Joan's perspective, and this was to be Robert's starting perspective. The second perspective for Robert however, was that despite this first assumption; individuals, and by extension the institutions that they create, can also become, things other than what they appear or claim to be. People as individuals can, in making the choices they do, betray themselves and those who rely upon them, as those representatives become corrupted by the short sighted vices of greed, laziness, vanity and hate, to name just a few; which may for them provide some immediate selfish artificial gratification, but in the long run are choices that are ultimately destructive to the development of themselves and humanity as well. Consequently, what Robert realized was that through the study of history, you could discover the true purpose behind the choices that people make (and have made), because with the passage of time, the actual true purposes of those choices (whether they be for good or for bad) become revealed through the results that are actually ultimately achieved. That is to say, that with the same precision that: for example, the rules of gambling undeniably stack the outcome of the gamble in favor of the dealer, and therefore makes the business of gambling mathematically worthwhile only for the house; so too does the outcome of most actions reveal the true design and purpose of the choices that people make. So when a particular choice of action leads to a particular result, then it is reasonable to assume that it was that particular result which was intended all along. And, when it comes to the affairs of man, (because such things are themselves manmade), to presume that such results are not intended, is to be as foolish as a person who walks into a casino believing he has an equal opportunity to win. Again, just as in gambling, although it may appear in the short term, that the dealer doesn't always win (because that's part of the rouse), the truth is that by design, in the end, the house always wins. And what Robert had learned through history is that although man's institutions were likely to make certain universal humanitarian claims, the actual true agenda behind those institutions, is always best revealed by seeing, and understanding, what final results are actually achieved.

So it was with this approach and understanding to history, that allowed Robert himself to succeed in school and some twenty years later, it was exactly this approach which gave Robert the teaching credentials to present such lessons to his own students in both political science and basic business law. In making the transition from student to teacher therefore, Robert endeavored to explain to his students that when evaluating the course of any particular set of human events, it was best to compare the events being studied through the eyeglass of the particular struggles that were supposedly being contended with (at any particular time), in contrast to the claims being made by the relevant authorities and institutions who were supposedly trying to fix those problems. As Robert would demonstrate, when you compare the actual outcome of those efforts being made with the claims that were being professed, consistently a glaring disparity would emerge between the solutions proposed (supposedly in order to fix the problem) and the ultimate results actually achieved. With those results (once you look past the claims being made), that a discernable altogether different long term agenda itself would be revealed as being the true pursuit from the very beginning. And again, to finish off with the gambling analogy, Robert would merely point out that the end goal of any casino is not the short-term outcome of any number of individual bets, or even the outcome of any series of bets; but rather, over the long haul, the more sophisticated agenda of the casino is to ultimately take all of the player's money, by simply keeping the player playing.

Teaching like this was why Robert was an automatic hit with his undergraduate students, because in the end Robert simply realized that the students were just craving to have someone tell them the truth. To the students, most of them the age of Maddi, Robert was the real deal, maybe because of his personal experiences as a young boy, or maybe simply from watching his mother trust herself (with a modest education) against all that she was being told. Whatever it was, to the students, Robert was a true believer, a real life "agent Fox Mulder." But where the fictional FBI agent sought the truth in obscure paranormal anomalies, Robert was simply able to point out (in his search for truth) that time and time again throughout history, what our public authorities were claiming and what was actually happening in America (and elsewhere) wasn't adding up.

But how bad was it? How far back, and how deep does this business of hidden agendas and betrayal go? Well again, for Robert the particular answer to this larger question was to be found in both history and psychology. Because the real answer as to when the history of human betrayal begins, or to understand to what depths it might reach, one must realize that the evil of betrayal is as old (and as contemporaneous) as man himself; because the first acts of betrayal are not those conscious acts of betrayal that we commit on one another (for they come later); but rather the first betrayals that occur are those betrayals that each man and woman perpetrate (consciously or subconsciously), on themselves. You see as Robert would explain it to his class: each of us go through our daily activities rationalizing and justifying our daily efforts as being either beneficial and/or necessary for ourselves, or for others. And as Geddy Lee points out: even though we may not consciously choose in each case which it is that we are choosing, in doing the action, "you still have made a choice." So what we must realize is that as we rationalize all that we do, all of our activities, all of our endeavors rationalizing them through our individual psyches; it is then through our psyches that we then grant ourselves certain indulgences (or excesses) that we then further rationalize as being either earned and/or even deserved. Or, selfishly we choose (deserved or not, consciously or not) to simply take… because we can. And when it comes to the issue of whether or not we have received such benefits honestly, because we must always be mindful that in the acquisition of all things there is always a cost to others. We need to question whether therefore, we truly addressed that cost; or did we engage in some form of willful blindness in deceiving ourselves as to the virtue in the acquisition of those things that we have taken. Such is the dilemma of man. Do we each have the courage and honesty to test our own self- justifying rationalizations (for all that we do, and all that we've done) to see if our rationalizations and justifications have gone far and deep enough; or do we simply surrender to the vices of selfishness, shortsightedness and convenience simply because we can. As Shakespeare reminds us "above all else, to thine own self be true." And it is with this question that one then realizes the true sinister (and political) evil that the act of betrayal actually performs generally, because it is the vices of man and his surrender to his excesses and vanity which pit an individual's actions, desires, pleasures and rationalizations; against the internal integrity, honesty, energy and sophistication of one's own potential self. Of course it is in one of our oldest stories of man, that it is the serpent's desire that we should actually surrender to our baser instincts so that the best of man should ultimately fail, or worse still, be defeated by a pathetic lethargy of denial that makes such a defeat all the more certain. And as Robert was apt to teach it, that from whatever historical book you choose, such betrayal is being contemporaneously played out by each of us, every day, as each of us gaze upon the apple of our eye, and contend (for that moment) with our own personal version of the "original sin."

Now at this point in his classes Robert has always been worried that his students would lose the message of history since so much of the historical evils of man have been so tied up with the acquisition of things. Robert felt that the students would come to see that the mere acquisition of things itself, as the actual demon that needs to be slayed most. But such is not the case; man's simple desire to better his condition in life through the acquisition of property and the creation of property rights, thus capitalism in its purest form; these are not the things that are the cause of man's folly. The simple principle that man should be allowed to keep, amass and dispose of that property which he creates, is of itself an intellectual vehicle that is no doubt a liberating force for both man and mankind as it serves to generate surplus and thereby separate man from being forever a mere beast of burden. Capitalism used in this way is but a tool to be utilized by man to provide increased wealth for both himself and others, and as a tool it cannot therefore possess any morality of its own. It can be neither viewed as a thing of virtue nor as a thing of evil. Property rights and capitalism therefore, properly understood (and in their least corruptible form), allow primarily for an economy of labor. It relieves a society from the need that each individual intrinsically be a jack-of-all-trades. Because the farmer can create a surplus of food, we need not all farm, because our carpenters can eat, we need not all build our own furniture, because there are desks and chairs, the efficiencies of schools and countless other industries are born. Capitalism in this way creates the opportunity for a multitude of enterprise and with it comes the "Wealth of Nations." The acquisition of things and capitalism as a driving force for production therefore, are not the cause of man's problems. It is man's use of the acquisition of things in order to elevate some and subjugate the rest, through the corruption of power distribution, which is the evil that is exploited through the creation of surplus. And again, surplus by itself, is just a thing, and things have no virtue. It is the use of surplus as a means of power, used as a weapon of control, and as an extension of vanity and ego. It is surplus used in the hands of vice, that makes another useful tool of man, a means of destruction.

So, oddly enough, because we can, because we can help or hurt, because we can make things, all sorts of things, and create other things such as surpluses; a choice for man in all things, is created. Because of man's conscious abilities therefore; man can, by virtue of our own intellect, choose to become more than what we are (regardless of what that more may entail) or; through our vices we can either (knowingly or unknowingly) aspire negatively in a direction that is in the end not only self-destructive to our individual sophistication and sensibilities; but in hurting ourselves (and others), we damage the evolution of humanity as well. And clearly when man or mankind, chooses to make those decisions that are universally positive in the results they achieve; we should not be surprised to see those who were responsible for making those decisions, readily willing to claim that such positive results were their true intent from the very beginning, because when man wants to be good, he can be good. But, when it turns out that those results have gone badly; where the final results conspicuously favor some to the obvious detriment of others; the question as to whether or not those same individuals are equally prepared to admit that they intended those costs to be imposed upon the unsuspecting masses from the very beginning, this question is then answered not by words, but (in truth) only by those who then actually try to remedy the harm immediately; thereby separating themselves from the pretenders who are simply content to continue the management of the harm deceitfully under some new pretext. Capitalism as a thing, and even gambling as a thing (which is really just the projection of mathematical probabilities); are just things in the hands of man, and by themselves therefore (just as things) they can hold no blame. But to be blunt, the corruptions of man therefore, can be readily seen to be played out every weekend, when some casino pit boss (knowing the mathematical certainty in favor of the house, in the use of long term play) says to the typical gambler, who has just stayed at the tables for the entire weekend, and lost everything: "well, that's too bad, but you have to admit, we did give you every opportunity to win."

When man's actions are intentionally rigged against the masses, in order to assist some and deny (or hurt) others, the question becomes whether the institution in question owes a sense of responsibility to those masses, or like a casino, because of some private relationship rational between a casino and its customers, it is free to play fast and loose with the truth and deny the damage which it actually creates. And although casinos are free to deny the damage that they do by placing the blame for a gamblers demise artificially on "the luck of the draw," or even on "lady luck" herself; and yet still further deny the damage they do outside the casino walls, in the form of latent addiction, depression, personal insolvency, bankruptcy and suicide, all under the pretext that the act of gambling is itself (despite whatever else one might think of it) nonetheless a voluntary, private, and contractual relationship. Therefore, as such, should be exempt from the contempt of the public. But as Robert would point out, that to see the privacy explanation as being the saving distinction to separate gambling from the other affairs of man, is to miss the point entirely. Because apart from the damage that institutional gambling does (privately) to individual gamblers; it is the underlying perfection of the practices of deception, denial and exploitation; that casino gambling puts on, in dramatic public display, demonstrating for all to see that such practices do indeed "pay." It is this, the lesson in deception, which proves that one can profit greatly by preying on the exploitation of others, which Robert points out, should be our greatest concern. Because with that out there, with it being proven consistently that deceit, denial and deflection pays off handsomely (for the house only); then for those who are at peace with the exploitation of others, there is then nothing to stop such individuals from adopting those practices into other private domains, or worse still employing them actively in the public domain.

So although it may be that through some abstracted concept of privatization, that we as a society find it privately permissible to allow the practices of deception, denial and deflection in such relationships as casino gambling to be used in order to make a quick buck; but after that, the question then becomes to what degree do we then allow for the transfer of these practices into other areas of our lives. Especially in those areas where the excuse that those deceived, did not volunteer nor did they choose to walk into the institution knowing that it was about to deceive them. One would think that where the element of choice is removed; that there would be extreme counter measures in place (in an accountable society) to combat the spread and use of such devices especially when it comes to the possibility that those same acts of exploitation are employed by our public authorities in their disproportionate manipulation of wealth (in favor of some) to the disadvantage and expense of the masses. Yet this is what Robert points out, to be routinely the case. And the curious historical question however, that Robert himself admits that he cannot seem to answer (when he reaches this point in his lectures) is which came first; did the art of politics (in millennium past) teach such sinister devices to the art of gambling, or did the sins of the dealer's house get adopted by the politics of man and get injected into the evolution of running the modern sovereign state. Unfortunately for Robert, as an academic question, it seems that both institutions are so sufficiently ancient (and their practices are also so similarly duplicated) that the question of which came first historically, is like the "chicken and the egg," an evolutionary dead heat.

But regardless of which came first, the point is made: and that is, for those who want to increase the wealth (and power) imbalances of the world, the mechanisms of deceit, denial, and deflection, are the automatic weapons of choice to assist in such ends. Especially, when in doing so you want to co-opt the engagement of the masses in their own demise. Why, because once the abuses of the manipulators become so obscene that their excesses exist for all to see, the beneficiaries and the status quo can then use these devices as weapons to immediately strike at the awakening psyche of the masses with the deliberate intent to destabilize and diffuse the masses before they can actually mobilize and articulate their anger at the root cause, namely the betrayal of the masses at the hands of the elite. These three destabilizing devices therefore are effective for the status quo because 1) through deceit (for instance) mass anger can be diffused by falsely alleging that such disparity is only "temporary" and that the current spike in inequity is "the result of unforeseen circumstances," due to "outside forces" or rationalizing that "with any systemic recalibration, the public ought to expect some momentary upheaval" and that with these particular spikes in wealth imbalance, well they "should in time self-correct." Or that through the use of 2) denial, the most recent disparity itself is just simply categorically denied, through such jingoisms as: "this current shift is not market wide;" and this disturbance is a "singular incident which ought to be seen as being isolated" and therefore this current imbalance is in no way "representative of a larger trend," or the ultimate denial of all, which is to say, that this isn't a case of exploitation at all, but rather this latest shift is an "inevitable reality," and so: "welcome to the new normal." And finally 3) deflection, where the disparity is most arrogantly blamed on the disadvantaged and the abused through the particular technique where some professional apologist for the status quo self-righteously proclaims that: "well the beautiful thing about it is that we live in a democracy so (if you don't like what's happening) then all you need do to fix this, is get out next time and vote." This is the most repugnant justification of all because it suggests that the people themselves are responsible for the latest extension of wealth disparity, rather than being the ones whom had it done to them. It's akin to the pit boss saying to the (now broke) gambler, "but sir, we are here because you brought us here, because with each bet you wagered, you have to admit the cards could have gone another way."

And in making this point to his class, (usually out of an urgent need to somehow lighten the mood); Robert would now make his infamous Eagles reference, and would explain that at this point in the comparison, the casino and the state analogy can be separated; because, in the case of a casino, not only do you at all times have the choice of stopping play by walking away from the table, but you can also step outside the casino and go for a smoke. But when it comes to the affairs of man, there is no stoppage of play (because the exploitation of you and the world, will go on without you/ because remember the government always has your social security number) and so when it comes to the affairs of the state, it is probably best (as Robert then explains) that we all see ourselves as the unwitting guests of the great Hotel California where it is understood that, because you are free, "yes": "you can check out any time you like, but (of course) you can never leave."

It is at this point that we find Maddi trying to grapple with her America, of today. You see up to now in her life, Maddi had been taught to see herself and her world much like her grandmother had done, where the average American is good and is trying to be good, much like the average American exists in many of Norman Rockwell's 1940's and 50's paintings. In fact, it was that very imagery that brought Joan and her family to America in the first place. It wasn't that Birmingham England was bad, it was just that after all the state corruption, betrayal and hatred (epitomized by the Nazi's) which had brought about the Second World War, Europe was simply bombed out and exhausted. So for a young family it made sense to try and get a fresh start in that part of the world where the ancient regional and ethnic divides just didn't seem to matter so much. And America, as Roosevelt and Rockwell had portrayed it, was still the land of opportunity. In fact, it was President Roosevelt's address to Congress in 1941 that inspired Rockwell's now famous Four Freedoms paintings, which were

Rockwell's take on the Freedom of Speech, Freedom of Worship, Freedom of Want and Freedom of Fear, that symbolized what the world could be, and what every father and mother should want for their children. You see the optimism for humanity that Roosevelt talked about, that Rockwell idealized, and the ideals the cynics and the skeptics criticized, weren't just myths, they were (and still are) a potential version of America that could be, an America that could be realistically aspired to because it did already exist (as a type of reality) in the hearts and minds of millions of individuals just like Joan, Susan and Maddi. And those were the visionary audience that Roosevelt and Rockwell were speaking to. The big question however (even back then and still with us today) is whether the emergence of that better America, ever had a fair chance to materialize under the constitutional regime that America has lived under for the past 240 years. That is, is it possible that we are finally realizing in the here and now (post 2000 AD), with the emergence of Maddi's generation and the new millennials, that we have in fact had it wrong all along and that the evolution of man and the evolution of America itself, has been deliberately and systematically retarded through our own dogmatic adherence to our own historic (representative) constitutional system. Is it possible that the U.S. Constitution, that we have all pledged our allegiance to, which is also supposedly the symbol of our liberty, has in fact been the legal anchor for a (representative) system that has chained America and Americans to only one way of life? That is, is it possible that the American constitutional system has, through its mechanical operations, turned out to serve a different agenda than the actual liberation of its citizens? Could it be in fact that it has been the Constitution, w h i c h has been mechanically used by our representatives to retard (if not prevent) our social evolution in the growth of our compassion, our intellect, and our perception and treatment of others. So dare we say it, could the adoption of our U.S. Constitution have been its own parlor trick? That is, could our constitution be like the casino, where the gambler doesn't always lose, and where the constitution (like the house) grants some periodic civil liberties (such as the achievement of the American Bill of Rights, or various heralded Supreme Court rulings such as Roe v. Wade, or Brown v. Board of Education); while its true historical purpose and design was to play for only a specified few, other than the majority of the people of the United States, in the pursuit of a more invisible larger prize, which was/ and still is, the continued (and evolving) generational betrayal and exploitation of the many, and the masses, for the benefit of an elite few.

Now in posing such questions as these to his students, Robert knew he was treading on hallowed ground; but with Maddi's generation and the new millennials, Robert was willing to gamble that things had changed; or at least, that the audience had changed. The paranoid purge of Senator Joseph McCarthy with his un- American communist witch hunt of the 1950's had already had its day and been rightfully exposed. Maddi's parents, Michael and Susan, although too young to have been at Woodstock themselves, grew up in its aftermath during the peace movements of the 1960's, where they witnessed firsthand, the student protests occurring all over America, including those four students shot dead by the National Guard at Kent State in Ohio protesting the Vietnam War in 1970. So for Maddi and all those who grew up in households like hers, with parents being wise and sympathetic to anti- establishment causes of the past, it made sense that such a generation would at least be open to discuss the historical evidence that Robert was suggesting. But as much as such sympathies could be relied upon from the historical protest movements of old, since the first days of Robert's teachings at the university at the turn of this millennium; it was clear to even Robert that ever since the great recession of 08, something else significant in the students had also changed. To the students who came in the semesters immediately after the stock market crash of September 29th of 08, and the economic carnage that came with its aftermath, there was from that point forward an ominous distinctly different sense of tension in the air, a foreboding quiet that was akin (as one colleague suggested) to the eerie quiet that befalls a stray dog, that once captured, strangely realizes that now in a clinic, he is to be euthanized. For these students, unlike the generations before them, where only specific segments of the people had been conspicuously abused due to the color of their skin, or because of their particular rung on the economic ladder, meant no escape from the draft; that for this particular generation, the millennials, that for them, their particular disposal was going to be on mass, and it was going to be bad. For these millennials, that with their massive student debts and their lack of future prospects, that they knew, that in their time, all the lies and hypocrisies of the past may have all finally come home and will now take their combined toll, leaving this generation with a tattered and exhausted American dream and the unflattering future nickname of being, if not the largest, ... then the latest: "generation screwed."

It is at this point in Robert's lectures, sensing the student's dismay (if not downright depression), that Robert has felt the need to demonstrate that although things appear to be bad, with the chaos and the dismal prospects on the horizon; that it is the very existence and recognition of a problem to be attacked that should give the students at least some cause for hope. Because if

America wants to truly be "the shining city on the hill," as President Reagan liked to idealize; and if in dealing with our challenges America truly does mechanically work, and if America is also truly "the home of the brave," then these challenges are ours (and theirs) to conquer. Now of course, every semester when Robert reaches this point, and makes the national anthem reference that he does, there is almost a universal on-que collective groan from his class as if to say all at once ... the national anthem, "really?" But what they don't realize is that this reaction is not only expected, but is in fact designed to raise the important question of when exactly does nostalgia become propaganda and how much propaganda is there in American rhetoric. Because if our national anthem is not a call for us to be brave against all enemies both foreign and domestic; and our anthem therefore is just a mindless emotional rallying cry for tribal purposes; and Americans are only to be brave in the face of foreign attack; then if that's all our anthem stands for, (and clearly millions like Hendrix have thought it to be more); then it is also true that President Bill Clinton was similarly just a false prophet when (during his inauguration) he called upon our domestic bravery in 1993 when he said "that there is nothing wrong with America that cannot be cured by what is right with America." So if both of the above are not absolute lies; then the purpose of our intellect ought to be to bravely discover what is actually wrong with America at its core. And if that is true, then It cannot be enough to merely only spot and diagnose the symptoms that plague America at any given moment (such as right now whether or not "black lives matter,"), complaining about the ills of the day (as Bill Clinton would have it characterized) from one generation to the next, for that is surely to be shortsighted, self- serving and, in the end, a prescription for disaster for us as a people. And again, if the text of the Constitution itself is to be treated seriously at all; when it declares in the preamble that our purpose is "to form a more perfect union, establish justice, insure domestic tranquility, ... promote the general welfare, secure the blessings of liberty to ourselves and our posterity," then if these words are not pure deceit, then the constitution itself ought not to be thought of as a document conceived only for the benefit of just a privileged few, nor ought it to be allowed to be (if deceit was part its original purpose) to be continuously used, as a means of oppression from one generation to the next. So even if the mechanics of our constitution allows for a deliberate method of social and political retardation and oppression, then if all of America is not a lie, at least let the glorifying principles that we refer to in our constitution, then let these principles be openly discussed, and let those discussions be the true representatives of what America could and should be. Unencumbered by our institutional deceit; even though we might have to accept that up to now the proactive tangible (legal) pursuit of those same principles have been routinely successfully defeated by the very same constitutional administration to which we are all (supposedly) chained.

Now in an effort to give the Constitution some hope, it is from this vantage point that Robert reminds us that in fact the founding principles of America (as mentioned in the preamble) may not actually be defeated as yet. For as Robert points out, that every Sunday, from the gospel churches throughout America, good Americans, practice and give life to a very real (though spiritual) form of patriotism, only because the pursuit of these same constitutional ideals have proven to be realistically denied to them, while actually being enjoyed (by design) only by a privileged few. And since this has indeed been the case, then a strong case can also be made that throughout our past, those millions of Americans who are best symbolized by the powerless black southern church parishioners, who praising the gospel from within their pew, and have enjoyed no justice for themselves, and yet who have persevered and survived the injustices of their time; that such unassuming individuals (by not turning their backs on America) have proven themselves to be more the American patriot, then many of our paid, empowered elected representatives, who have claimed the same. And at this point, almost as if to make a footnote to his own lecture, (and ... to make the point that the truth is indeed out there) Robert refers his students back to the specific words of Bill Clinton to show that Clinton himself may have completely understood the betrayal that was, (and still is) going on; when he recognized indirectly that there is indeed a two tier approach or method, to the overall American pursuit of our evolutionary cause. What Robert points to is that in his inaugural speech, when Clinton professed that the "wrong(s)" of America needed to be "cured" (as opposed to being "fixed,") by that which is "right with America;" Clinton was specifically recognizing that the "wrong(s)" of America could be corrected by those things which are right with America, namely such things as free speech, decency and true patriotism. The very same virtues that were (and are) symbolic of a better America ... the very America that could still be, ... the same America that was epitomized by Roosevelt, Rockwell, Reagan, and millions of unassuming church faithful, ... not to mention the "more perfect" America that already exists in the heads of the likes of Joan, Susan and Maddi. In doing this, Clinton was directly acknowledging that the good (people of America) could still overcome the bad (the selfish and those who are content to

33

betray and exploit others) if they could just mobilize themselves somehow and teach the bad, the error of their ways.

The problem with this call to action however was the very real betrayal that Clinton himself was then about to commit. By deliberately characterizing the "wrong(s)" of America as things which needed to be "cured" as opposed to being things that needed to be "fixed"; in choosing the word "cured," Clinton chose to deliberately mislead the people, because as America's "wrong(s)" were to be deemed as illnesses, such illnesses carry with them neither intend nor blame, while man made machines designed to hurt and oppress can be used for both. Put simply, illnesses have no purposes or agenda's, but man-made machines can be made to have both.

So when Clinton chose to characterize American wrongs as things in need of a "cure," what he accomplished with that characterization was that he successfully removed himself from the responsibility of having to fix the very machine that made him President. Consequently, with this characterization that the "wrong(s)" of America were (and are) in need of a cure, Clinton was also deliberately and clearly deflecting back to the masses, forcing the responsibility for finding those "cure(s)" back onto a (unstructured and nebulous) populist who without their Presidents help, would have to search out such cures or fixes, for themselves. And this characterization was sinister enough, because it was none other than our own Commander in Chief therefore, who was himself putting the burden for fixing the largest issues facing America, back on to an unorganized body, namely the American people. And what Clinton knew, from the very moment of his inauguration, was that the only single representative that the people had (as the people had just elected their President, Chief Executive Officer and Commander in Chief) was him. So rather than recognize that there were things that could be institutionally fixed through strong leadership, Clinton having been entrusted with the people's office, refused to acknowledge that there were such mechanical things that needed to be fixed. Consequently, the operation of the people's single most powerful representative within the Constitution, saw the due diligence of that office itself break down on Clinton's watch, because Clinton himself simply refused to acknowledge his responsibility to be the good people's institutional advocate for mechanical change under the current system.

Or to put it another way: Clinton became President by working with the rich and the established status quo, and so on the day of his inauguration he chose not to open the debate about whether the constitution and the system itself may be at fault for the perpetuation of the "wrong(s)" in America, because he was already beholden to the elite for what he was about to receive; namely (having now taken a bite from the apple), for his silence (and his deflection), he was now to be awarded the keys to the White House. Clinton's hypocrisy therefore, on his very first day of office, was to show how that which is "right with America;" namely the power of free speech itself, could be institutionally defeated, bought off, ignored, or even denied in the actual halls of power so much so... that the pursuit of reform through the freedom of speech could only take place realistically, as an informal and unstructured matter outside the institutions of government and therefore outside the structure of the constitution. Consequently, what Clinton did on that day, was he deliberately exiled (under his watch) any discussion about structurally reforming America, relegating any such discussion to the place where it could do the least harm, and that was outside the system itself, banishing such discussions from the halls of power, and in his case the Oval Office, leaving free speech to be only theoretically practiced in the living rooms, class rooms, coffee houses and churches, etc. of America.

And the extreme irony of Clinton's inaugural speech, is that the statement that Clinton has now made most famous for himself, is therefore now nothing more than a propagandist deflection; a misleading form of immense American rhetoric in the maintenance (and pursuit) of the way things already are. So to be blunt, what Clinton did on the first day of his Presidency, was to implicitly say: 'Hey America, join me and lets renew the promise of America; meaning I will work with Congress to try and improve (through legislation only) the economy and I'll initiate legislation that will assist and ease the pain for as many as I can; ...but on the bigger issues as to who is actually running the show, and by what means do the elite inflict their harm and maintain their strangle hold on the oppressed ...yea well, on those larger, more corrupt and deceptive issues ...you can get back to me on that, when you have mobilized a wave of support for reform that I (and my established friends) can later co-opt, manage and again take advantage of, ... so yes, when you get to that point ... you give me a call, America.'

So if our politicians won't honestly identify what is wrong with America, or when they do, they choose only to react to the latest and most visible casualties, like a triage unit, tending only to the immediately injured (usually for the purposes of buying for more time) because they know, that with everything; … everything eventually becomes yesterday's news. And if, as Clinton's political maneuvering suggests, that the big issues are to be left to the people (in their classrooms, coffee shops, dining rooms, churches, etc.) then okay: in order to separate ourselves from the pretenders; then let us (says Robert) ask here and now, the big question which is: what is wrong with America, … at its core?

Now of course at this point in Robert's lectures, as he hits this question, not only does an immediate silence befall the auditorium, but eye contact with each student is instantaneously reestablished as each student looks up suddenly from their laptops as if they expect to see some sort of magic trick, and the reason that Robert is the recipient of such sudden prairie dog attention is again because the students want to see if somebody is actually going to tell them the truth. And Robert, for his part, is just smart enough to realize that now he has commandeered their attention on this very sensitive (if not violent) issue, where truth challenges propaganda, Robert knows that from here on in, that all the attention he gets for the rest of this class, next week's class and the weeks thereafter; not to mention all future prospects for being re-hired next semester (or any semester after that) now depends on just how close, to accurately answering this question … Robert can actually get.

So what is wrong with America? Well although the easy answer would be to say that there is a lack of vision and courageous leadership, Robert warns however that there is no shortage of courage in America. Clearly our armed forces and first responders, they alone (not to mention countless other groups and selfless individuals) prove that to us on a daily basis; so there is no shortage of courage in America. And on leadership, well there too in every platoon, rookie class, grade school, high school, college, community center and on every training ground, ball park, ice rink, player's field, shop floor, kitchen, auditorium, dance studio, recital hall, and what have you; leadership too (like courage) abounds in America. The best of it coming from the simple mentorship within the smallest of groups, where the lost and confused find real strength in the honesty, humility and dignity of those who choose simply to reach out directly to others. But again this sort of courage and this sort of leadership is of the populist (extra constitutional) kind. It is the apolitical leadership and courage of the average working American. It is the bravery and leadership that comes from non- political virtues based on decency, kindness, respect and upbringing. It comes from knowing the difference between right and wrong, and choosing to make that choice part of one's daily routine; and this type of courage and leadership has nothing to do with politics, philosophical, institutional or otherwise. This kind of bravery and leadership comes out of being a good person. It comes from understanding the virtues of hard work (and not just profits), it comes from understanding the point behind an honest hand shake, and a willingness to look someone in the eye for the purpose of demonstrating integrity and commitment. It comes from a genuine concern for one's neighbor, and the belief that just simple decency should be extended to all people, regardless of their nationality. ... And it is these Americans that have been exiled from Washington, by those who are already established and corrupted, who once in power stand guard at the constitutional gates.

But then the question becomes: if there is so much bravery, courage and leadership in America, how can it be that there is still so much that is "wrong with America?" That is to say, if all (the good things) that have just been said about America, are true; then why hasn't more of the best of America (its bravery, courage, leadership and decency / as those characteristics are backed by our sheer numbers) spilled over democratically into the institutional operation of America? In short, if America is so good, why is Washington so impenetrable? And if "we the people" are in charge (because we live in a democracy) then why hasn't Washington done more to fix things? And, the short answer is: because "We the People" have never been in charge, and worse still, we were never supposed to be (or at least never supposed to be immediately or contemporaneously) in charge; and that's the true parlor trick, the deception that by allowing us to choose or change the puppets, that such an electoral process means that the puppets matter and therefore, we matter. When the truth is however, that the puppets (when properly understood) are all really of the same stripe; and that therefore our exercise of our democratic / constitutional methods, ... are also really of little or no consequence.

So the truth is that for the great majority of us, those of us who are good, but live on the outside of the halls of power; that even if we succeed in sending in one of our own, that the rich and powerful who are already on the inside (because they have always been there), because disguised as representative of us they wrote the constitutional mechanism that would continue to protect them; that they see us the "good" (and our potential shepherds) as naïve entities to be brought into line. And historically, this has been the legacy of representative government from the very beginning; and therefore the battle between liberty and oppression has always been built on a sinister time delay, where the history of all oppressive "wrong(s)" (as Clinton characterized them) have been legally sustained to their individual breaking points, to be endured by the oppressed to the point that the abuse is no longer tolerable and something has to give. Then, and only then, does real change actually occur. So, if one is a Clinton supporter, then at best you would have to justify Clinton's inaugural speech (if not an actual betrayal) as a concession speech, where (supposedly as one of us) he simply chose to reduce his Presidency from the very start, to being that of a mere custodial manager for the status quo, thereby abandoning the masses who voted for him, in their true fight, abandoning them in their hopes and dreams that as our Chief, he would have done more.

So, it's not that oppression and exploitation aren't with us in the here and now, that's the whole point: they are (both of them), both exploitation and oppression are with us all of the time, because these two evils have been with us, right from the very beginning. It's just whether or not the current particular oppression or "wrongs" of our day are overt or visible enough, to have actually reached their boiling point. And one would think that in a civilized (first world) nation such as our own, that we would have no reason to celebrate a peaceful transition of power (on policy matters alone) from one governmental administration to the next, unless of course it is understood that it is our own laws and representatives who are actually behind the maintenance of what is currently wrong with America, to begin with. So instead of saying: "Hey America, let's find a way to rethink things so that your wishes cannot be betrayed," we find instead at every inauguration, our new Commander in Chief celebrating once again in their speech another peaceful transition of power, because the truth is that since the people are not in charge, that this time once again the current oppression and exploitation through the establishment, has been sufficiently managed or hidden so as to ensure that the current unrest has (yet again) not been pushed too far. So when those Presidents who choose to be mere managers, talk of "sacrifice," what they are really saying is that those of you who have been denied; … that your suffering and patience in the meantime has been greatly appreciated by those who have benefitted and enriched themselves as usual … and who themselves, as usual, have sacrificed nothing.

So the question then becomes (in the modern era) whether the people themselves in America are aware enough of what abuse is actually taking place at any given time. And so increasingly the purpose of a government that is hell bent on maintaining the privileges of the most select few, must by design, therefore, push its abusive operations and techniques, forever further out of sight or underground. Consequently, routine elections (from a privileged perspective) become useful in their most superficial form, not to bring about any real change but rather to create the appearance of democratic control when in fact what the elite and the oppressors are really looking for is a helpful pressure gauge to measure the extent of our nation's awareness and tolerance for those particular abuses that are currently taking place.

So where we, the masses, are told every four years on January 20th to rejoice in the celebration of this regiment because it demonstrates that "we the people" are still in charge, but we the American people have to remind ourselves that historically the term "we" has always been a highly selective and exclusionary term. And what we might have just witnessed, on any given January 20th. is the exchange of puppet villains in order to calm our mass frustrations; for those who would exploit the masses further by resetting their tactics and continuing their play of us ... from a new, and undisclosed, vantage point. This is why the battle for liberty has always been both in the past and in the here and now, because as times change, where awareness is raised, and abuses are exposed, and where tolerances have been exhausted; those who want to better their position in life at the expense of others, push us to our limits to see just how much more they can get out of us, simply because ... they can. For example, President Obama recently commented that freed slaves technically got the vote, after the Civil War, but that all women still did not get the vote for some further 50 years later, not until 1920; and yet President Obama when commenting on this very fact chose not to expose such oppressive retardation of human evolution as a mechanical flaw that was deliberate by design, but rather spun the issue as one of celebration for the perseverance that it was. The simple truth is that our Constitution isn't designed to stop change, its purpose is only to slow down the rate of change so that those in power can stay (as best they can) out in front of it. And our Constitution for its part is again blindly celebrated by the majority of us, because we get so caught up in the euphoria of a peaceful transition and the appearance that we ourselves have somehow effected some sort of change, (albeit at that moment only a celebrity or ceremonial change), that we lose sight of the fact that we have been played yet again. Convincing us once again (to stay at the tables as it were) and give our abusers still yet another chance (where the system is rigged against us) to allow them to continue whatever hidden agendas, abuses and injustices that are taking place during our time. All the while, we (like the foolish gambler) spend the next four years in the hopes that this time, "real change" (as candidate Obama personally promised) would come for us, ... this time, for sure. And with such representations as these, the battle then continues from one generation to the next, where our current tolerance and knowledge about the truth of the abuse of our time, is tested against the propaganda and the rhetoric of the puppets and the puppeteers who are content to push such abuse to the point of exhaustion and to extremes because (mechanically)...they can. Meanwhile the masses enjoy only their hope for liberty from the abuse of the day, that justice for them will come someday; thereby forever pivoting the American people in a never ending battle of ... "us vs. them." What is most sinister however, about a society that adopts such a detached generational approach for reform and justice, is that a society that is so patient for progress is itself also a society that silently regards its current populous with contempt, as those who innocently believe in the system are abandoned and left to suffer with their pain. Only to realize later, when the results of time are tallied, that all along in the eyes of the establishment, that they the masses, "the (majority) people of the United States of America;" were/and are, both individually and collectively, expendable in their grief as they are disposable commodities for the extent of their lifetime. And when the control of the privileged should become so exposed so that such control cannot be had for much longer; then it is to be maintained at the instructions of the elite for as long as possible through the betrayal of our representatives in the legislation that they pass, so that the benefits of the way things are; ... are maintained for the elite (hopefully) for the duration of their lifetimes.

So to be blunt, our Constitution when it starts out with the most famous three words in history: "We the People", created mechanically (both back in 1789 and from that point forward), in real time, an apparatus that would allow for the maintenance of two entirely different types of people, the people who would be empowered to legally exploit and abuse other people, and the 'other people', the masses; who by the measure of the first (for any number of reasons, such as race, gender, etc.) are by design to be those people to be played, betrayed, and taken advantage of.

So what we have to recognize is that our founding Constitution was built with two deliberate and separate operating agendas. The first is its inspirational representations that the Constitution is historically most famous for (cynically let's call that the carrot), which includes the revolutionary idea that the document itself is a creation of "the people," and as such that its founding purpose was (and still is) to establish justice, insure tranquility and provide for the general welfare and secure liberty, for those same "people." But the second agenda of that same document, the subtext agenda of our Constitution, the hidden agenda (this we can call the harness for the rest) which was (and still is) to allow for the convenient retardation and delay of liberty, through exclusion and exploitation of all the other individuals. And this purpose was made abundantly clear from the very beginning, when at the time of its adoption it excluded the vast and the many, (numbering more than half the known population at that time); through its legal enforcement of slavery and its legal exclusion, exploitation and oppression of all women. In addition to these two more notable exclusions were other individuals who were deemed to be similarly inferior and subordinate (or

44

entirely disposable) as they existed as indentured servants, the property-less, the working poor, the unemployed and the destitute; and all other individuals who were either viewed to be simply unworthy, or who were unacceptable (for any number of other reasons) to be granted their inclusion to the legislative rights and privileges of the "(other, more worthy) people." And the significance of this dual purpose agenda (though unflattering as it may be) cannot be overstated because with it we can see the actual legal adoption of a designed, deliberate and institutionalized human hypocrisy set upon to purposefully betray the masses, millions of them, not only for the purposes of exclusion but also for the far more corrupt purposes of exploiting them physically (through their labor, their needs, their youth and their innocence, while also taking advantage of their strength, their hopes and their dreams); all for the personal gain of an advantaged few that elevates an already privileged class to an even higher (material) socioeconomic stratosphere.

And again, the most sinister aspect of this process occurs because it is not only our own representatives who are taking advantage of the unassuming masses, but also our fellow countrymen, who as citizens (both back then and currently), wish to elevate themselves on the backs of others. This all taking place, because the peaceful masses are only looking to live their lives according to the virtues and promises that were taught to them by their parent's in their keeping of their beliefs and ideals. The same beliefs and ideals of life, liberty and the pursuit of happiness, which were supposedly the cause to our great fight for Independence; and those same stipulated values as embraced in the preamble of our Constitution. All of which have been hypocritically preyed upon, time and again, by our publicly elected representatives who in their pursuit of public office, public authority, and who for themselves, reap the benefit from the power and esteem that comes from gaining control over the distribution of our public purse.

So the U.S. Constitution therefore is by design the architectural structure that supports both the nebulous potential of a visionary, and evolutionary liberty; while it simultaneously institutionalizes and allows for the continued (mechanical) manipulated oppression and exploitation of those who would exclude, control, and even 'own' other human beings. The human vices and negative character traits therefore that were the underpinnings for the rationale of state sanctioned slavery didn't just, after thousands of years, disappear with the passing of the Thirteenth Amendment. Those among us who had (and have) the character traits to be comfortable with overt forms of extreme human abuse and exploitation as epitomized through the original recognition of slavery; with time, just adapted and shifted their designs of exploitation into more sophisticated and progressively more covert means of control and subjugation, as they stayed ahead of the awakening (apolitical and trusting) populous. So once the Constitution was amended to stop its most overt form of legalized exploitation (namely slavery); those among us who were (and are) comfortable with such tactics for human exploitation; did from that point forward, simply engage more and more in the art of underground and covert betrayal, to once again sustain the endless battle of "us vs. them." So just as slavery gave way to the Jim Crow laws and segregation, and industrialization in the north took us from colonial agrarian serfdom to sweat shops and urban poverty; so too (says Robert) do the millennials at this time in our nation's commitment to globalization, do the millennials have good reason to look back at history, and question: what exactly do they "(those) people," those who have given us generational genocide, and a tortured and murderous historical past ... what do those people, now have instore for the millennials?

From the Magna Carta to the One Percent

Of course Maddi had heard her uncle Robert's rants before, usually during the holidays at Thanksgiving and Christmas, when her mother Susan was determined to make sure that her bachelor brother had a place to go every year for the holidays. And when Maddi had listened to Robert's concerns back in Oak Valley while in her middle teens, although somewhat interested, she felt that such matters were so academic and distant, historically distant (not to mention horribly sad and boring); that she felt she was entitled to, if not ignore what was being said, at least she thought she'd be excused for being what she was, which was to be a teenager with the problems and concerns of a teenager. And at that point in her life, that's exactly what Michael and Susan also wanted most for their daughter. But with New York City now on the horizon, in school or not; Maddi's future was now upon her.

Now the great thing about New York City is that there is such a buzz in just being out and about, being in the coffee houses and the restaurants, amongst the crowds and the sky scrapers, that its physically exciting just to be outside. So using any excuse to do more than just go to class, Maddi would look for any chance she could to go out and do things like shop and see things, but mostly she just enjoyed being out amongst the crowds in the midst of the hustle and bustle of whatever was going on. Just walking anywhere was fun to do because although she didn't know, really anyone, there was of course always the chance of bumping into other students or meeting people through other acquaintances; or (like in the movies) there was always the hope that she would meet someone fascinating in a bookstore, or by happenstance while simply browsing, or (best of all) by just turning a corner. So, mischievously, ... every chance she got, Maddi was out the door.

So in the hopes of always meeting new people, Maddi would make excuses to meet up with her uncle Robert because although he could be a bit of a killjoy if he got going on one of his sermons, she knew he was legitimately worried about things (not to mention that he was usually right); and besides when she was with him, she got into the coolest places because first of all he had more money than she did, and because as an ADA ... he knew all the cops, ... and some of them were, well ... kinda hot.

So, routinely (apart from other times) Maddi would try to meet up with Robert most Saturdays for brunch and this was good fun because it got her out of bed on a Saturday (when depending on the night before, she might not have otherwise); and apart from getting a free meal out of her dear old uncle, Robert would sometimes have something pretty cool going on that night that he would always try to include her if she thought she might be interested. So hang'in out with the 'old guy' wasn't so bad.

And so it was on one September Saturday, that when Robert called to give Maddi her usual helpful wake up call, that this time Robert called to have her meet him in a different part of town rather than their usual greasy spoon strip. Oddly this time, Robert had asked her to join him at Franklin's Bistro down in the financial district and as she was just waking up, she was jarred from her morning fog when he gave her the name and address, and advised her to wear something different than her usual jeans. Something was up, but if she was going to make it by 11:30, as requested; she also knew she'd have to scramble.

As Maddi's cab pulled up, Franklin's was definitely posh. The front doors alone were twelve feet tall and filled with intricately beveled glass. Clearly, these eggs were going to be expensive. As she entered she was immediately greeted by an elegant hostess who somehow spontaneously inquired: "Maddi?" To which Maddi nodded. "Your uncle is this way."

Uncle Robert was seated at table by a towering window, which, from a distance, Maddi could see looked out over a beautiful patio. As the hostess was escorting her, Uncle Robert was talking in a very familiar way with (a really good looking) waiter who was pouring him a glass of water. Upon reaching the table, Robert stood up, they both exchanged their customary kisses to the cheek, and out of the blue, dear old uncle just blurted it out: Oh Maddi; this is Patrick, he's my TA, this year, for my political science class." … And the jig was up.

Now as set-ups go, this was a good one. Patrick was tall(ish) and as his name suggested his family was Irish … and to the extent that he had a noticeable accent however, Maddi couldn't tell, how much … Irish.

Once the pleasantries were over, Maddi was able to get the scoop on Patrick. Patrick was an Irish American working on his Master's degree at NYU, but he did his undergraduate degree at Trinity College in Dublin getting his specialty in political psychology. According to Robert he was insightful and his thesis in subconscious predispositions looked promising, the big question was how quickly he was going to transition his work into a Ph.D. Patrick's great grandparents were immigrants to New York in 1926 and although his parents were born American citizens, his family went back to Ireland often enough, that when offered a full scholarship to Trinity College in Dublin for his undergraduate degree, he took it. And with such familiarity with his ancestral homeland, Patrick was therefore a decidedly proud (Irish) American.

Maddi was ok with her Uncle's not so subtle, efforts; his motives being that since she was new to town, he thought it a good idea for her to meet others closer to her own age, and who Robert could vouch for as being neither a promiscuous cop, nor (as best he knew) a chainsaw killer. And since Susan (as it turned out) had given Robert the necessary matriarchal approval to make the introduction. Maddi from her perspective (and since he was quite good looking), ...and since it was true that she was relatively new to the city, ... how was Maddi to complain.

What Maddi didn't know however, was that her Uncle had already gone over the top and asked Patrick if he would take Maddi to Les Misérables, relieving him of two tickets (he somehow came in possession of) set for the Thursday next. Patrick seemed to know all about the tickets but it was news to Maddi, and when her Uncle told her at the table in front of Patrick, she was (situationally) allowed to be legitimately embarrassed, while silently being grateful for having gotten the awkward formality of actually getting a date, out of the way. So the arrangements were made, numbers exchanged and the dinner and show were on.

Thursday came and there Patrick was in a bowtie and tweed sport jacket leaning against a cab as Maddi came down the steps of her apartment. In the cab on the way to dinner of course Maddi feigned the audacity of her uncle's arrangements and probed more into how Patrick and Robert met and what were Patrick's career plans with a political science degree. To this Patrick, confidently asserted he wasn't sure about his future plans, but that at present he found his studies fascinating and since he had a full scholarship and he was getting by on his tips from the restaurant and his teaching assistant money, ...that since his parents were happy, he felt that at twenty three he could take some time to see how things go.

Dinner was at a little café/ pizzeria in walking distance to the theatre, but you still needed a reservation and of course Patrick had made all the necessary arrangements, including a table with a street window view. Maddi took note of the effort that Patrick had made and although she wanted to know more about him and his family she thought she would try to keep the conversation more neutral and objective to start, so the safe place to start with was with his studies. So she started:

"So Patrick, why politics? I understand why my uncle is so obsessed, because clearly ... he has issues; but what is it about politics that made you go into political science? And ... oh yea; please explain to me why they call it political science anyway? Because politics seems to me to be the least scientific thing in the whole world? Isn't politics really just about power, ... and money, and getting elected just so that you get more of both; ... not to mention titles, limousine services and mansions? "Well," he responded, with a laugh, "You're right, it is about all of those things, but to answer

52

your first question first. For myself, I always wanted to understand why things are the way that they are. I always wanted to know how things worked, and the more I was taught, the deeper my understanding became, so for me personally, right now I'm on a journey into human political psychology, because sometimes it can be pretty cool: trying to look into someone's mind, because you never quite know where it's going to take you. And as for the other things; again your right, politics can be trivialized with an emphasis on the superficial trappings that comes with political ceremony and scandal, but for me politics is a window into the true identities of individuals, groups, and even nation's; … realizing of course that the window itself (due to such things as a false sense of history, propaganda or some undisclosed hidden agendas) may give us a distorted picture of what we are actually looking at. For me right now, I'm focusing on two different aspects about politics, first I'm trying to discern which reliable fundamentals exist in politics, like the periodic table is the basis of chemistry, and then once those building blocks are discovered, to see if they can be mechanically harnessed as positive fundamentals for purposes of future appropriate and justifiable decision making. And as far as whether politics can ever be viewed as a science or not, well whether it's a science or an art, like the debate over economics, I'd say the jury is still out on the both of those issues. Oh and when you were chronicling the superficial, (Patrick adds with a smirk and a wink) don't forget to include the cocktail parties and the gossip, … they're the best part. And so the conversation started, pizza to share was ordered, and at Maddi's insistence; because he seemed quite genuine, she encouraged him to continue, so Patrick explained:

You see, as far as understanding the fundamentals for both law and politics, once you strip away all the trappings both are quite simple, and it can be boiled down to starting at, or revolving around, one thing, and that one thing is: who in the end has the legitimate use of brute force. The use of brute force is the key to understanding everything about all nation states and societies. Put simply, because man is a physical being he has the random power "to take" anything at any time. Why, because man as a physical being has control over whatever brute force his body can muster, but because we are all physical beings we are also all mortal and regardless of how strong any one particular individual may be, all of us live in the physical reality where each of us have to acknowledge our own vulnerability; which remains with each of us, all of us, ... all of the time. So even the strongest among us are completely vulnerable against the use of brute force when confronted by either superior numbers or by treachery, as we are all at our most vulnerable when we are either unaware of what's coming, or ... when we eat and sleep. So strength itself is not a complete defense against someone else's choice to resort to brute force against us, because no one can be on their guard against the aggressions of another all of the time. So the answer to the use of random (or individual) brute force is the certainty of consequence for those who might attempt to use it. So the nation state exists in its most primitive form to impose both reprisal and consequence (around the clock) upon anyone who themselves would resort to the arbitrary use of force against anyone else. So the nation state is the answer to the arbitrary use of brute force, because by having all brute force concentrated into one final chain of command (ergo a single Commander in Chief) all individuals can relinquish their own use of brute force because it is safer to live under the dictates of one single authoritarian figure than it is to live in a state of anarchy, where the power to take or, the power to kill; can at any moment be boiled down to nothing more than "any (random) might, makes right."

Now you have to understand, that by relinquishing one's right to resort to brute force (whether by choice as supposedly in the United States; or not, as in the case of a dictatorship) to a single authority figure or representative; does not mean that such a society has achieved justice, it only means that a society so based will have a rough approximation of some sort of "order." Consequently, by placing the power "to take" all things (including one's "life, liberty and the pursuit of happiness") into one overseeing body, a society makes the use of brute force orderly, … and with order, the use of brute force at least becomes somewhat predictable. And knowing who has the final ability to ultimately "take" all things is the key to stability and security. "Justice," in turn, then becomes the goal to be pursued once order is in place. Justice and order therefore are not the same thing. Order is simply a means to an end, because with the establishment of order comes security, and with security comes the luxury of moral debate. And with moral debate comes the luxury (in a physical world, where all things can be taken away) of answering the more cerebral of all questions such as: what is Justice. And so as a people go about perfecting their own concept of justice, so too (supposedly) does their society become less violent, because in a just society, (so the thinking goes) fewer individuals have reason or occasion to reclaim their (original) right to resort to their own use of physical force. Consequently, the most 'just' society (apart from foreign attack), therefore ought to be, the most stable society.

Once the pizza was done a quick look at the time and both Patrick and Maddi realized they'd have to hurry if they were to make their seats. And as the theatre lights went down and center stage received the spotlight, the story of Les Mis took over for the night with the sad plight of those who had to endure post-revolutionary chaos of 19th century France with its depiction of poverty, love, internal conflict and hardship causing those themes to resonate with Maddi in a more profound way given the raw political discussion about the harsh realities of human existence that she and Patrick had just had.

Anyway, two days later on Saturday morning, Maddi was oddly motivated to meet up with her Uncle to carry on with the abstract discussion that she had started with Patrick to see what Robert's thoughts were historically, with the concepts that Patrick had conveyed, which seemed to make the theater performance far more real than just an amazing musical. So, eager to thank him for the tickets and an incredible evening, that Saturday she met Robert with a kind of historical curiosity of how what she had seen portrayed on stage, had any bearing beyond France. So as they waited in their booth for their strawberries and pancakes to arrive, after telling Robert about as much as she could about the evening she had just had; in the hopes that Robert might give her more to contribute the next time she was to meet up with Patrick (which by arrangement was going to be that very evening), she did the unusual thing, and actually asked her Uncle to explain to her how politically things got to be the way they are. And with such a direct request, Robert was more than happy to oblige.

So how did it all begin? Well the modern western nation state of course goes back to the Roman Empire, which was founded originally by Roman military occupation and conquest, but changed for the west with the fall of the Roman Empire, which occurred because on top of its Barbarian difficulties, as an occupying army it had become overextended, both geographically and financially, and therefore collapsed leaving the modern western countries of today (such as England) to develop in its aftermath as sovereign (royal territorial) realms or kingdoms. Now after the Roman legions finally left, within what we call the British Isles, numerous Kingdoms evolved amongst the various differing regions. And of these competing kingdoms, the one king that did the most to solidify what we now call England was King Alfred the Great and the reigns of his son Edward and grandson Aethelstan which went up to 939 AD. After that, the English throne changed hands but a few more times until the Battle of Hastings in 1066, when William of Normandy also known as William the Conqueror, seized the English throne and took charge. And this conquest was particularly significant because not only did it usher in a new lineage of Monarchs but it also led to William ordering the compilation of the Doomsday Book which was to provide a precise assessment of what each person and household held in assets (such as land, servants, slaves, livestock, produce, etc.); all for the determination henceforth of what future taxes were to be paid to the protection and administration of the realm. Hence the name: Doomsday Book, because once in it, nothing but doom lay ahead for all those who were to be taxed according to it. So with the Battle of Hastings and the tabulation of the Doomsday Book, a stark point of clarity about human existence can be discerned from both of these events, and that point of harsh reality is that: with the command of superior brute force, in the absence of justice, one begets the servitude of all beneath … and with that servitude, to those in charge, goes all the spoils.

Now the thing about Kings enforcing their own right to rule

through their command of brute force is that in order to maintain such military might, all kings had to rely on the loyalty of their most trusted subjects as they would send them out as administrators to enforce the king's decrees to maintain the King's control over his claimed domain against foreign invaders and domestic rebellion. To do this the King had to bestow title, privilege and properties in exchange for loyalty, obedience and the deliverance of taxes to the King's treasury. Thus in order to extend a King's realm to its furthest territorial reaches the King had to create an elevated elite, an aristocracy of wealth, title and privilege which subjugated all other subjects to the service of just a chosen few. And in a medieval world, where by todays measure few physical comforts existed, leaving all to live a rather harsh existence with few material benefits, in such a world raising the elevation of personal status through class stratification and an abundance of personal servants (not to mention the depths to which that service might go) made the significance of class stratification and discrimination, the center piece of civilized society. So to answer the question as to how this all began ... well (so as not to be too crude) but in order to make a long story short: ... that's how.

So as taxation goes: census in 1086AD., with the Doomsday Book; and considering what had always existed before, namely: the exploitation of the masses through various forms of servitude (crucifixions aside), the beginnings of the modern day nation state takes on a more formalized (almost consumer index) approach in further objectifying its constituency (from that point forward) for nothing more than the fiscal benefits and advancement of a select few. But of parallel importance, what was also taking place at this same time, was that: as this chosen form of stratification (a class based society with the aristocracy at the top) could be counted upon to ensure order of the masses through brutality and the extraction of taxes; so too did that same aristocracy come to realize its own appreciation and awareness for its part in maintaining the strength and financial prowess of the King and the fiscal maintenance of the realm. And as the realm was to grow either in size or in undertaking (such as in its own defense or in the extravagant pursuit of the Crusades) so too did the King's dependence grow upon (what was originally) his chosen few. So with time, and the increasing demands of all things; came a material shift in reliance which would ultimately transform, and lead to, a shift in power. And this economic strain and shift between the King and the chosen few allowed for (an invisible) separation in the King's own grip in command over his own chosen delegates. Giving early cause (to what would later become a historical trend) in the demands of (what was to come later) namely a thing called Parliament (which loosely translated means: to "speak," or have a 'discussion').

And so it was, that by the year of 1215AD.; that the Barons holding numerous grievances against the King, forced the king to give his seal to a commitment within a document, called the: Magna Carta (the Great Charter), which was basically a peace accord after a rebellious faction had risen up and seized the city of London, where the King acknowledged that any new taxation of certain types would only occur (against the nobles only) if it had their input and counsel. This Charter therefore later became (through folklore mostly) a symbol: that a pact does indeed exist between a sovereign (the state) and its people, that the former rules over the latter with the consent of the people. Now this was not at all what was expressed in the Great Charter, but again (through mostly folklore) this is what was born from the mythology of the Magna Carta as that mythology was to evolve into a political ideology, even though the original peace accord (the Magna Carta) itself failed to keep the peace. Why, because once the threat was gone, and the rebel grip on London no longer appeared to hang in the balance, the King reneged on the commitments made within the accord, and the realm was plunged (within a year) into civil war. But of great hidden importance with this folklore was the propagandist notion that whatever was accomplished (by the rebel Barons) was that their victory, as much as it was, was a victory for the people. But the truth is that, it wasn't that at all. The Magna Carta had little if not nothing to do with the people writ large, the masses; its promises (if there were any) were reserved for the nobles, and the freemen only, and were not undertakings made towards the population at large. In short it was a deal made between the king who held the legal symbol of authority (the ultimate right to use brute force during peace time) and an elite group (the aristocracy), the two of which who had supposedly agreed (from the Magna Carta on) to work in concert, according to law, in ruling over the masses. In short, the Magna Carta had nothing to do with liberating the people, rather it more just legally recognized that the establishment, were supposedly from that point forward, to be included at the table of power, with the King, in determining the future of everyone else. The Barons weren't representing the people, they were representing themselves, in a deliberate (legal) effort to maintain their elevated separation from the people. And this separation due to title and rank was for the further purpose that they might (in a more formal arrangement with the King) continue their combined future rule ... over the people.

And of course approximately four hundred years after the sealing of the Magna Charta, during the reign of Charles I, the momentum of this idea was to be put to the test. What had happened in the meantime was that in the furtherance of administering the various shires and counties the freemen would choose (nominate or elect) other members from their local or region to sit in the 'discussion' as to how best to run things. However, in the early 1600's, King Charles, faced with a hostile Parliament, chose to suspend the debates of the "people's' representatives by closing the doors of Parliament indefinitely. And although this was not a direct violation of what was agreed to in the Magna Carta, throughout the realm over those four centuries the idea of what that document (and the folklore surrounding it) stood for had grown sufficiently in the minds of the commoners (in a predominantly illiterate society) to allow Oliver Cromwell to champion the supposed principles of the Magna Charta and raise a civilian army of sufficient strength to overthrow the king's forces and to later hold Charles to account for what Cromwell maintained was an act of treason.

Upon his defeat however, King Charles refused to acknowledge that he held any obligations to his realm's people or Parliament, maintaining instead that his right to rule was of a divine nature and that as king he need answer only to God. Since he would not retreat from this position, and since Cromwell — who now held the greatest physical force, namely the loyalty of the civilian army (which through conquest had laid claim to the legitimate use of brute force) — had Charles I executed for his defiance and for his crimes against the realm.

With the beheading of their king, however England was to immerse itself into a constitutional crisis. The recognized holder of brute force had been removed by brute force, leaving a constitutional vacuum. But since Cromwell had overthrown the monarch in the name of the people and their perceived constitution, he was able to receive the title that as Lord Protector of the Commonwealth he would be the defender of the realm, and he promised to stand guard by virtue of his rank as commander of the civilian army and to maintain order until the constitutional question of who (or what institution or office) in the place of the king should ultimately have executive command over the use of brute force. Unfortunately, Cromwell however was to die of natural causes before this issue could be resolved, and with his death, England — faced with the prospect of descending into a chaotic spiral of fracturing rivalry— chose instead to invite Charles II (who was in exile in Europe) to retake the throne on the understanding however that the ability of the king to suspend Parliament indefinitely was not what the British constitution stood for. And confronted with the prospect that he might never regain the throne by any other means, Charles II supposedly agreed to such terms, and as a consequence the monarchy and the aristocracy were re-established in 1660.

Now constitutionally when discussing the events that led up to the republican era of what is now Great Britain, much has been said about the constitutional crisis that came with Cromwell and the British Civil Wars, but more importantly is the further development within the Western democratic myth, which is the fallacy that with Parliament's and Cromwell's fight against the despotism of King Charles I, and with the concessions that were to follow, plus the other reforms of the 1600's, from the Glorious Revolution of William and Mary and the passing of the British Bill of Rights of 1688. That these, so called accomplishments, demonstrate that representative government that followed was in fact an instrument of "the people." The democratic suggestion was that Parliament was becoming ever more inclusive of the common man as it were, when in reality such reforms were more representative of the rise of the "untitled" *moneyed* class within the Commons which were taking on ever greater prominence through their sheer acquired wealth, and their corrupt control (and ownership) of such things as the "Rotten" and "Pocket Boroughs" (pocket meaning that the MP was beholden to a financial patron who had him in his 'pocket' per se') within the House of Commons. What was happening was that although the Common's representatives were part of the King's Parliament dating back to the 13th century, they were just one of three to five groups within the King's Parliament, which went from little significance in the 13th century, to much greater prominence due to their increased wealth as merchants and traders. Consequently, their accumulated wealth posed as a major source of tax revenue that was vulnerable to the taxation whims of King and Parliament, so like their predecessors, the aristocracy, the newly rich demanded that (their wealth be better acknowledged) in order that they might better minimize that which they (the *nouveau riche*) might lose through the powers of taxation. So with their escalating affluence, the wealthy interests of the Commons representatives, successfully commandeered for themselves, in the name of the people a predominant place at the sovereign's taxation table. The fact that the Commons itself, with its rotten boroughs, pocket boroughs and its larger denial of the right to vote, was anything but representative of the people within the entire constituency didn't seem to matter, because with the propaganda of the past (and a name like the Commons…) the truth itself, just didn't seem to matter.

And the democratic myth that this third inclusion was somehow representative of a populist movement became solidified simply because these so-called untitled increasingly affluent commoners (who gained their financial influence mostly through mercantile trade and commerce) were perceived to be (because of their lack of title) of a lesser status and therefore "representative" of the larger population. The truth being however, was that just because representative government was expanding to include a larger number of untitled representatives, did not mean that the (economic) priorities of those same representatives were the economic priorities of the much larger (less financially significant) population within their constituency. In fact, it didn't mean that they were representative of them at all. Even Cromwell being an elected Member of Parliament who took up the cause against an absolute Monarch (for religious and tax reasons) who amongst others was successful in having the House of Lords abolished by Parliament; did not, or was not able to secure for the larger masses, a Parliament for the masses; even though there was a movement at that time called the Levellers who were prepared to rebel in order to get a greater distribution of wealth. So powerful however, were the moneyed interests within the House of Commons by that time, that within only two years of Cromwell's death did that same Parliament (which had been freed of a despotic King and an institutionalized aristocracy), choose itself to reinstate both the Monarchy (in Charles II) and the aristocracy with the resurrection of the House of Lords. Why, because on its own, the moneyed   class within Parliament's (House of Commons) would be on its own against the masses which it was supposed to symbolize (but didn't), while also being threatened by an ousted aristocracy and an exiled Monarchy, all at the same time. But with Parliament reinstating the House of Lords and the Monarchy, it could in conjunction with the nobility and the king, all three working together; could go back to the familiar infrastructure that existed before, where Parliament could continue to look like it was protecting the people against the visibly powerful, while the House in drafting all future tax legislation could ensure that their particular interests (that being the moneyed interests of industry, family and friends) could have their tax consequences conveniently spared (by legal exception), minimized, or even ... overlooked altogether. Consequently, the history of wealth disparity goes back at least as far as the origins of Kingdoms and realms (and realistically could be seen within the Roman Empire) but more important to the evolution of the west, is the falsehood that representative legislatures democratic or not, evolved as representatives of an entire constituency, when the truth is that these bodies used their powers of exclusion to instigate some of the most extreme forms of oppression and slavery to enhance their wealth, precisely at the expense of the majority. ... The wealth disparity therefore of today is a direct (though highly more evolved) descendent of this detachment, while the hypocrisy that western legislative bodies are the servants of the masses as opposed to being beholden to the extreme financial powers (or the 1%) within, is a most convenient relic of propaganda that has survived, and been successfully co-opted by the democratic myth for centuries.

History Repeats Itself for the Fourth and Fifth Time.

Now of course the story of the Magna Charta (and all the reforms that followed) cannot be limited to the history of Great Britain, because generally the story of the Magna Charta can be used as a historical digest of just how a nation state (under a constitutional structure) that employs a representative government, can simultaneously work at cross purposes between supposedly representing all, … while actually working most (and best) for only a select few. And of course, it was precisely this sort of double-dealing, which was again attempted by the greed of the moneyed class in Great Britain, which, actually lead to the grievances, and events in 1776 with the Thirteen Colonies.

What happened in America leading up to the American Revolution was that with the reign of King George III, the British Parliament chose to repay the debts resulting from the French and Indian Wars by securing the necessary funds through legislation of a series of taxes to be imposed almost exclusively on the constituents of the various American colonies. This legislation was passed by the British Parliament, which was comprised of only elected officials from the constituents of Great Britain and therefore there was no representation from the constituents of the American colonies. Yet through a series of statutes, such as the Declaratory Act of 1766, King George and the British Parliament were quite prepared to proclaim for themselves the overriding authority to pass all laws with respect to the colonies "in all cases whatsoever." Such a dictatorial stance infuriated the collective intellect of the colonists, who saw themselves as equals to their British counterparts. The glaring inequity of having no control over the taxes to be forced upon the American colonists gave cause to the great American revolutionary cry that there "shall be no taxation without representation" and to the idea that to tolerate such a regime would be to defile the 'rights of Englishmen' as developed since the time of the Magna Carta.

Moreover, it was just this sort of inequality that Thomas Jefferson was to denounce when as one of the chief architects of our much famed Declaration of Independence, he wrote: *"We hold these truths to be self-evident, that all men are created equal, that they are endowed by their Creator with certain unalienable Rights..."* Just as important, the Declaration of Independence also went on to state: *"That to secure these rights, Governments are instituted among Men, deriving their just powers from the consent of the governed, — That whenever any Form of Government becomes destructive of these ends, it is the Right of the People to alter or abolish it, and to institute new Government, laying its foundation on such principles, and organizing its powers in such form, as to them will seem most likely to effect their Safety and Happiness."*

And of course the principle that Jefferson and the other signatories were supposedly most interested in, was establishing the political mechanism for responsible government: the very concept that a government with "just powers" is a government ultimately accountable to its constituency. But herein lies the ultimate hypocrisy. As the Declaration of Independence itself points out, the very abuses of brute force that gave rise to the American Revolutionary War came about while the British realm was a practicing democracy. In Great Britain's renowned House of Commons, its own elected members of Parliament had themselves passed the much-despised tax legislation *precisely because* the colonies had no representation while still within and under the jurisdictional authority of the British sovereign. The obvious hypocritical betrayal felt by the elected representatives in the thirteen colonies — who were attempting to manage their own regional municipalities by practicing the very same tradition of British representative democracy so long fought for — instead found themselves disenfranchised and powerless to resist the laws enacted by their British counterparts. It became apparent to all of the thirteen colonies that when dealing with the human reality of self-interest and the issue of raw power, that once one tastes the intoxicating ability *to take*, the abuses and corruption that may follow cannot be restricted to kings (or even aristocracies) alone. Jefferson and the other signatories recognized and stated as much when, in concluding their grievances as set out against King George in the Declaration of Independence, they felt compelled to point out, *"Nor have We been wanting in attentions to our British brethren. ... We have appealed to their native justice...to disavow these usurpations,. ... They too have been deaf to the voice of justice and of consanguinity."* (Consanguinity, meaning: people who are descendants of the same ancestor.)

So what we see with the events leading up to the American Revolution is that those who had the legal authority to take were willing to do so despite the glaring inequity that to do so was to take advantage of those who were just simply vulnerable to their legal authority. And it mattered not (to the British) whether they were doing it to individuals who were every bit their equal, nor did it seem to matter that in each case it would be done under extreme protest. All that seemed to matter was whether the ability to take advantage of other individuals ... was there; and if it was ... then it would be done, simply because ... it could be done. Consequently, history repeats itself for the fourth time. Just as the King through conquest 1) used the masses to his own ends, bringing about the revolt behind the Magna Carta; and 2) the aristocracy after the Magna Carta brought about their own demise with the rise of Cromwell; and 3) with the re-established Monarchy and aristocracy, Parliament (as a whole now dominated by the nouveau riche), chose to collude in the oppression of their own disenfranchised domestic constituents; and so to next did 4) Parliament again repeat itself, as it abandoned its offshore Brethren in the colonies. ... Such is the legacy of representative government (despotic or otherwise); and so too, apparently, ... is it the legacy of representative democracy, as well.

So despite the fact that the American Forefathers were to speak of loftier goals, and despite the fact that they themselves had just been betrayed, abandoned and disenfranchised by their fellow countrymen, our Forefathers in what has been called the Great American experiment, set out to create a new nation founded on the high principles of equality and justice, but as did their British predecessors, our Forefathers failed themselves, by giving in to the worst of themselves. In defining their new collective, like their earlier British counterparts, they selfishly chose to restrict the definition of equality so as to empower some, much to the extreme detriment of the many. Empowered, were the American equivalent of their own moneyed interests — predominantly white, property-owning males — at the time leaving most white males, almost all blacks and females to have no say in this new realm of self-government.[1] The establishment of a more representative form of democracy did not therefore

---

1 At the time of the Revolution the Founding Fathers were content to leave the right to vote in the hands of the individual states therefore there was only four states at that time that extended the vote to free blacks.

---

automatically secure the reality of a constituent's equality in the pursuit of self-determination, even though the Revolutionary War had just been fought on that very principle. The stronger human reality that those who hold the power of the state (that is, the power *to take*) will 5) selfishly try to hold on to it (so that they can exploit others), to the exclusion of others (all others); proved once again to rear its ugly head, and made this human trait, the dominant trait, of those who pursued a life in American politics. So, for the fifth time, the human weakness that embraced human servitude, exclusion and oppression, which had already taken root on colonial soil (as Americans were to take advantage of their own); proved itself, within the American experiment, to be more powerful than the glorified principles of justice and equality of which our Forefathers spoke.

Fundamentally, then, if we stand back and look at the historical lessons of the West as played out in Great Britain and America up to the 18th century, we see that when it comes to the business of administering the hopes and dreams of man, instituting order for the benefit of just a select few, is in fact the overriding, yet hidden, true consequence and result (and therefore also the true agenda) for the creation of the representative state. And although in each of the 17th, 18th, 19th, and 20th centuries specific moments and instances of populous progression in the pursuit of liberty can be found, and dwelled upon, if one's purpose is to glorify the western state; but if one does not have a predetermined propagandist purpose to their analysis, then one can see that without exception that with each so called liberating accomplishment there are countless groups and millions of individuals who are conspicuously left out and left behind, sometimes for the very purpose of deliberately replacing those lowly individuals who have now been supposedly liberated. At the time of the American Revolution, the abolitionist movement was well underway, and hotly contested at the time of drafting the US Constitution, and yet at the behest of those who simply wanted to profit further from slavery, slavery was written into the US Constitution, despite the self-evident truths proclaimed in the Declaration of Independence. And, in the battle for gender equality, this struggle too, had its first proponents long before the patient and arduous success of the suffragette movement. Abigail Adams, for instance, the wife of President John Adams was already a strong advocate for women's rights in education and their right to own property, pushing for such things long before and during their stay in the office of the Presidency, still within the 1700's.

One might argue however, that despite the protests of these times that somehow the persons responsible for the perpetuation of these injustices and those who acquiesced in their continuation, were themselves somehow less culpable than their apparent hypocrisies would make them out to be; the lame argument being that they were just products of their time, that to have asked them to have done more, would have been to put what they did accomplish, at risk. The argument being that, to have asked our Forefathers to have done more, would have been to put the very union of the United States in jeopardy. That the southern states would have never signed on to a Constitution that outlawed slavery, and that it isn't fair to put (anything close) to modern day expectations for gender equality on an 18th century patriarchal dominated society. That to measure the achievements of our Forefathers, in either the United States or in Great Britain; to measure such leaders by what they didn't achieve is to be unrealistic and to be a "dreamer." That to make such a suggestion, is to be disassociated from the realistic possibilities available at that time, because such aspirations were not only logistically impossible, but also simply beyond the mass comprehension of the general population during those times. Such arguments will tell us (in a pathetic deflection) that during those times, it was in fact the ignorance and beliefs of the masses themselves that made the greater liberation of the oppressed impossible. But if all of these defenses are to be maintained (as opposed to being exposed for being the pathetic deceitful justifications for keeping things the way they were [and are], ...by keeping true reform outside the halls of power) then let us also recognize through our honesty and our intelligence, that it must then also be pointed out, that with these explanations justifications and defenses relied upon and put forward by our leaders, ...that such defenses expose equally that in the eyes of our leaders (both past and present), that the oppressed masses of each generation were/are, and always have been, the expendable and disposable commodities to the political elite for each generation throughout time (Obama included). Otherwise, if we weren't, or are not now, expendable and disposable commodities in their eyes, then given their immense suffering, beatings and murders; then more could have, and should have, been done (again Obama included). This is the true agenda behind the western representative state, it is a society built on creating a harnessing structure that retards and impedes the progress of human justice, deliberately asking us to live our lives surviving on isolated incidents of small and brief victories while all along those in charge (like the casino) take everything else. It is a system that pushes the discussion of reform to the outside to see if an awareness and a momentum of sustained discontent is at hand, in order that it can then jump out and undermine its purpose before it can gain momentum. Or if change is at hand, then it is a system well designed to delay the implementation of any change to the next generation, thereby preserving the privilege and wealth that the elite currently enjoy, while providing the elite through the control of the legislature the most immediate control over regulating, impeding and retarding the rate of change that is to come.

And as Patrick was to explain to Maddi, which was Robert's point all along; that the diabolical genius behind the western representative state is that it successfully makes western failures for liberty, invisible; because … they simply never happened. All that is tangible and visible to see is the change that is allowed to occur, not visible is the change that would have been best (or even the change that was most necessary) because those changes never occurred at all; why, because they were never allowed into the halls of power in the first place, not even to be debated. And all that our leaders ask for, in our historical analysis (and in the glorification of "their historical achievements") is our complicit and convenient forgetfulness (as a society) of the suffering and pain of those lost generations (being millions upon millions of individuals) who paid the actual price of our leader's neglect, hypocrisy and injustice, in the

73

meantime. The American and Western constitutional system survives as it does because it does nothing to self-correct. The burden is put on outsiders to pry change from the hands of the establishment. So not only does the establishment (and our leaders) wait for the casualties to occur, but then it allows those casualties to pile up to see if there will be a champion amongst them to force justice upon the establishment. All the while allowing a huge reservoir of anger and discontent to build, just so the establishment can see how this discontent is manifesting into something that at some point, down the road, such grievances might require a token gesture towards justice, just to release some of its steam.

And as an aside, as to the larger question as to whether the US Constitution (or any western constitution for that matter) is a by definition a mechanism for deceit? Well, it is interesting to remember that one of the founding colonies to become one of the original Thirteen of these United States, New Hampshire; which has sustained a state motto of: "Live Free or Die," would continue to believe (even if it had been content with such a manipulated definition of freedom at the time of Union), that by today's standards, that the constituents of New Hampshire would maintain that they are truly free, when they realize that their freedom (and even their ability to intellectually define their own sense of freedom) is restricted to someone else's (hidden) and manipulated terms. Because you can never be free, when your freedom is secretly defined by someone else.

Enslaving Freedom Of Thought, To One Way Of Life And The Mechanization Of Betrayal

So three years had come and gone, and Maddi was feeling quite the New Yorker. She now had her favorite hotspots and her own group of friends, mostly class mates, and of course there was Patrick who had turned out to be great, but he was always trying to work on his thesis. Patrick had finished his Masters between Maddi's sophomore and junior year and was now into his third year of his doctoral program, and most importantly he'd met mom and dad, (already) two Thanksgivings ago, and they seemed to like him, ... so that was good. But now it was her fourth year, Maddi knew that she'd be graduating with a Bachelor's degree in Business, with a major in marketing and a respectable, but not great, GPA. So that too was good, but from there she had no idea where she was going. The seniors in her program didn't seem to be finding any jobs in their field, despite the fact that everyone (in the media) was saying that there was quarterly job growth out there. Occasionally, Maddi would pay attention to the news between preparing lunches for her and Patrick (she enjoyed surprising him with amazing sandwiches) and preparing her term papers; and she noticed that the news anchors, in reading off their teleprompters always seemed to sound so upbeat about the national employment rate and the general state of the economy. But somehow in their enthusiasm, these statistical reports always made Maddi feel suspicious. Sometimes, Maddi felt while watching such economic reports that (after critiquing their hair and outfits) that their corporate read of newly minted government reports was little different than the few clips she had seen of North Korean anchorwomen spinning that nation's nonsense. Either way, like Tokyo Rose before them, the agenda of such self-serving economic reports, left Maddi more confused than well informed, so she didn't trust them. And yes, this is what three years with Patrick and Robert (and twelve courses in corporate marketing) had done to her, Maddi was now a true blue, bona fide, healthy American skeptic. Maddi was now learned in the way of the "sale." The sale of everything ... including the truth; and yes, even the truth about our own history.

Now when it came to the truth, one thing is for sure, and that is that after spending three years in New York and dating Patrick in the meantime, Maddi wasn't a teenager any more. Her appreciation for the workings of the world were now much more sophisticated due to her schooling and the company she kept. And to their credit, Patrick and Robert when put together were not only enlightening, but they frequently gave cause for Maddi (through their banter) to pause and rethink things (sometimes even the simplest of things) from a whole new perspective. For example, (just like the nerds which sometimes they were), both Robert and Patrick would entertain themselves in social settings by discussing famous movie quotes as if there was a secret conversation going on between Hollywood and the rest of America. Robert would usually start the conversation by bringing up a quote and asking for Patrick to give his opinion, just to see if Patrick thought it had any significance. And sometimes for a laugh, the subject would be silly and pure nonsense, and other times ... not so much. For instance, in the movie: 'Shooter,' when the corrupt Senator is trying to give Mark Wahlberg a reality check as to how the world really works, he turns and says to Wahlberg: "there are no Sunnis, and Shiites, there are no Democrats or Republicans; there are only 'the haves' and the 'have nots.'" And Robert's take on this quote, is that if anyone said something like this in anything but in a fictional setting, you would probably attract far more attention than any real person (or any politician) would like to receive, and yet there may be more truth in this statement than anyone would like to admit. Or, on a lighter note, in the movie: 'The Hunt for Red October,' in the scene where the President's NSA Advisor is confronting Alec Baldwin about the possibility of a Russian defection, the NSA Advisor acknowledges confidentially that: "I'm a politician, which means that I'm a cheat and a liar, and that means that when I'm not kissing babies, I'm stealing their lollipops, but it also means that I keep my options open…" And when the NSA Advisor then suggests that Baldwin go himself out into the frigid North Atlantic Sea to investigate the probability of this defection, Baldwin responds to the suggestion that the Advisor chose him because: "You…" and Baldwin interjects, "are expendable," and to this, the President's Advisor responds, candidly: "yea… somethin like that." And although Maddi realizes that both Robert and Patrick don't take themselves too seriously when they muse about the actual truth in fiction; the thought that some movies are obviously more than just fictional entertainment, has caused Maddi to watch movies more closely to see if the movie makers are trying to provide any real insights into people generally, or that they might actually be trying to tell us what's really going on. Patrick once commented, during one of these debates, that It's like the old adage in comedy that: "it's funny … because it's true." A funny joke or a good movie quote may not always be true, but the point that the guys were making (in their recurring banter) is that in today's world, there may be more truth in a good joke or a strong movie quote, than any one wants to admit. George Orwell wrote both books, Animal Farm and 1984, for a reason; and he wrote them *the way he did* for a reason as well; so could it be that we have now already started down a road where there is more truth to be had currently (even about the subject of free speech itself) in fictional books about barnyard animals and espionage movies, than there is truth … in any of the guarantees of the First Amendment?

So now with three years under her belt, Maddi was well versed in the art of the sale, and that in making a sale it isn't so much the product that you're selling that makes the sale, but more how the sale makes the buyer feel, that makes the sale. The product in the end isn't as important in closing the deal as the image that the buyer gets of him or herself if he buys the product. The product in order to make the sale can therefore be a thin veneer of what it purports to be if in the end the image of the thing is (really) all that the customer is looking for. That's why chrome looking plastic on various car parts is the manufacturers choice of material instead of chrome metal itself because (with most new cars) it's the image of chrome plated parts that is the desired effect not necessarily the material itself that the buyer wants. And that's why as well, beautiful high heels (in women's shoes) that are painful to walk in, still fly off the shelf. So sometimes in sales it's the psychology of the thing that is most important provided however that the substance of the thing itself is not someday put to the test to see if its real or not. Such was the theme in Maddi's course, 'The Psychology of the Sale,' a course which she enjoyed very much because one of the subthemes (that she liked to concentrate on), was the marketing objective of trying to enhance the value of the product through the process of making the product assist the buyer in feeling better about themselves. This was something Maddi thought she would be good at because she felt she had a vision for things; and that maybe someday she might look for a job in interior design work, artistic packaging ... or maybe even, try her hand at home sale staging. Maddi thought that she might be good at home sale staging because she had always dreamed about fantastic homes and she always thought she'd be good at showing people what a home (with them in it) could look like.

Anyway, Maddi liked the subject of psychology as it had been introduced to her through her marketing courses, and it was also something that she felt she and Patrick had in common and it gave them an academic reference point to talk things through; and admittedly she would sometimes mischievously use the subject to try and gain insight as to how Patrick saw the world because individually, she and he would come at the subject from such entirely different perspectives. Maddi's personal perspective (despite the fact that her background was in corporate psychology which clearly almost always had an oblique motive) saw psychology as a means of helping people in any number of positive ways such as seeing a given space in a whole new way or to see how to approach a problem from an entirely different point of view. While Patrick on the other hand, though he himself too wanted to help people, would discuss psychology more from a detached analytical (political) perspective where: how people reasoned, or how people viewed themselves, was more something to be left as it was; because as a political manipulative tool, psychology (was something to be objectified) in order that it could be used to predict future behavior and thereby used as a means of political control, or possibly, even used as a potential weapon.

Such a display of these two totally different perspectives would occasionally become self-evident in the most spontaneous and unexpected ways; as it did the one time when Maddi believing she was asking a simple enough question (with regards to the British referendum as to whether the UK should leave the European Union); asked Patrick as to why generally western democracies don't use referendums more often? And she asked this because she had always felt that referendums just seemed to be a reasonable way for a nation to resolve some of its biggest issues; but also secretly she was curious (since her grandmother was British) whether Patrick harbored any ill feelings (being of an Irish background and all) towards the UK, or England in particular. But what she got as an answer was something she didn't expect at all, which was a mechanical almost robotic answer that was completely devoid of passion or emotion for the nationalistic issue that was at hand. Patrick's answer was that: direct democracy (through the use of such mechanisms as referendums) is rarely used in western democracies because the business of empowering the voters is not what a representative state is all about. Patrick explained that from a political psychology perspective the typical voter is best kept under control, and therefore more easily used and potentially exploited, if he or she is left as they are, which is primarily responding and behaving as a: "two- dimensional person."

Now as insulting and as offensive as this appeared, Patrick went on to explain (as if it were a simple matter of fact) that from a political perspective the average person can be broken down (as to how they see themselves and how they behave politically) into three predictable dimensions. The first is how a person most readily rationalizes their existence through acquiring and defining their own particular sense of identity. This first dimension starts with their name and the places and people they believe they belong to, such as their family, their family associations, their employment, their religion, where they live, what their most personal hopes and dreams are, and probably, finally their stipulated nationality. The first dimension is therefore probably best understood as pure "identity" tribalism, in its most basic form.

The second dimension within the typical human psyche (again from a strictly political perspective, as Patrick would caution, as if to distance himself from the very repugnancy of what he was actually saying) is more relationship driven, it is measured by the actual people that each individual meets and interacts with. It is a separate dimension because although it stems from the first, it is representative more of the strength of the ties in the relationships made, the bond between husband and wife and family, and the difference between friends, close friends and mere acquaintances. It is the dimension that is reflective of the people you actually come in contact with, the one's you spend the most time with, and even the ones you pass by, but still meet, in the most fleeting of ways. This is the dimension that preoccupies our psyche the most, because it is the most demanding. It is here that our most immediate responsibilities occur because it is here where our direct and spontaneous consequences are realized. Have we paid the rent or the mortgage? Is he or she going to leave me? Are the kids ok? Am I going to get fired? What are the results of the biopsy? These are the major concerns of the second dimension, while this dimension also includes such lesser concerns as to whether or not the repair man or cable guy will arrive on time.

The third dimension however (from a political perspective) is the goal that is up for grabs, it is that part of our lives that deals with our public affairs. The third dimension is the part of our consciousness that deals with our place on this earth as we consciously realize that we leave a physical (and a public) foot print as we occupy time and space and as we consume oxygen and natural resources. It is this dimension, which acknowledges our impact on other individuals of this earth, even though we have never met, nor are we likely to ever meet, any of them. It is that part of our awareness that tells us that there are concerns beyond ourselves (the first dimension); and beyond the people we know and meet (the second dimension); that concerns us (possibly directly but not necessarily) where our control over such things are however probably neither day to day, nor to be seen immediately at hand. It is our more abstracted concerns over such things as our

Justice system, national defense, border patrol, our education system, social welfare, our transportation, and sewage system, the regulation of our telecommunications industry, the regulation and protection of our environment, and the list continues; the third dimension of our consciousness is therefore all of these things and more; because we realize that in one way or another, their management does, or can, affect us directly. But we also realize that they are all things that are not in our immediate (or personal) control. And because they are beyond our sense of immediacy, either because such concerns are so numerous themselves; or, due of their complexity they are beyond our immediate ability to comprehend; or, because they are simply beyond our personal reach, these concerns are considered delegated (or "taken," depending on your point of view) by our so called caretakers (or representatives) that are supposed to put the public's interests (our interests, at least according to the democratic myth) as a top priority in the management of each of these concerns.

But herein lies the betrayal, because the evolution of the representative state has never been (even from its original inception) about what is best for the people (the majority of people), the real system has always been instead about the privileged maintaining their status and position (and later "nouveau" wealth) in contrast to the masses. Rather, the representative state has always had a predominant competing agenda with the best interests of the people, because it has always been trying to maintain its separation from the people. And because there has always been a predominant (yet hidden) conflict of interest in this regard (despite all the hypocritical representations of liberty, justice and equality to the contrary), between what the system claims for its people and what it is actually doing to them, the system of representative government has therefore always been about betrayal first and accountability second. So as to the question as to why there hasn't been more referendum generally, well the truth is that the people were never actually supposed to have access or control over their own public agenda from the very beginning.

Patrick then pointed out that this is why he wanted to work with Robert to begin with, because of Robert's known emphasis on history. Patrick's point is that, Robert has been the most precise (of those who are discussing such things) in explaining that when representative government began, control over the public domain was seized and commandeered by brute force, leaving all liberty and justice (and all management over this third dimension including the question as to which issues and concerns are to be even included in this third dimension) to be at the complete disposal and discretion of the only authorized representative to use brute force namely: the sovereign, the King of the realm. Then slowly out of the need of efficacy and administrative efficiency in order to successfully exploit and expand did the reaches of the sovereign grow from one, namely with the King, to an aristocracy, and from there to an entitled (but not "titled") nouveau mercantile rich, and from there it went to colonialism (till that went bust), then it went to what we see today which (in other nations) are oligarchies and plutocracies, or what is called here in the United States the corporate agenda of the ultra-rich (or the 1%). And even here in the creation of the United States, when in 1787 the Philadelphia Convention first drafted the US Constitution, it was drafted by America's wealthiest who were content to exclude most of our own American constituency because they (the lesser souls) were taught and told that they weren't worthy of being included in a nation's governance that was supposedly founded by: "We the People."

So just like the privileged few who saw fit to re-establish the

Monarchy in Great Britain in 1660 after Cromwell, in order that the newly rich could themselves be protected from unwanted taxation, yet simultaneously join in in the ranks of oppression of the greater masses; so too did our American Forefathers give in to the worst of themselves by restricting the definition of "We the People." Our American Forefathers didn't initiate the American Revolution because they were opposed to oppression or disenfranchisement, they compelled the revolution so that (they themselves) America's elite, would not become the oppressed. All for the exact same reasons that they might continue slavery for the south, and while allowing the north to continue with the further oppression, exclusion and exploitation of whomever they saw fit. So direct democracy or populist democracy has never been an option, because it's never been part of the plan, … that is the real plan; which, as it turns out, is exactly the same plan (minus the titled aristocracy and Monarchy) on both sides of the ocean. To get any form of populist democracy therefore, as a matter of right in Washington, would require another Philadelphia Convention and (as Bill Clinton's Presidency reminded us) … 'that ain't gonna happen.' So this was Patrick's answer to Maddi's simple question as to why there aren't more referendums. And though stunned and grateful for the explanation that she had just received, she was at the end of it, … well, … exhausted. But then that too, that exhaustion (encouraging us to therefore remain within our two-dimensional perspective of our own pursuit of happiness), has always been part of the overall (representative) plan as well.

Maddi took a few days to ponder what Patrick had said. It was important to her because the more she thought about it the more it bothered her. It bothered her because she didn't like to think about herself as being two dimensional and although she had never given the functioning of democracy much thought before, she always knew that politicians and the powers that be, kept things from the public; but to deliberately and to directly manipulate things so as to encourage people to become intellectually oblivious (in their own demise) ... to Maddi that was something else. So now Maddi could begin to understand why, when she once met Patrick after his tutorial for Robert's course, she could see in numerous desk tops, the carved graffiti nickname of: "The Conversation from Hell," because not only did Robert's classes deal with some of the darkest hidden purposes behind the very creation of the United States, but Maddi too was beginning to grasp the numerous hypocritical (and mind interfering) betrayals that have taken place, not to mention all the human suffering that has occurred as a direct result, and all of this ... kinda made her feel a little bit ill. Also, Maddi couldn't get it out of her head that it had never been suggested to her by anyone ... that our system itself, by encouraging her to relinquish her personal connection to public affairs, could be knowingly dumbing down her faculties and her actual intellect for appreciating the same. For the first time, Maddi now saw the typical pre-election push to get the "vote out" as a hallow pretense in contrast to the false (propagandist) imagery that request conveniently creates. Of course voting was/and will always will be, important; but it should be important on a personal and a multi-dimensional level, not important in the same one-dimensional way that paying one's taxes is important, or renewing one's passport is important. Although voting is a civic duty, it's also much more than a civic duty. If properly understood (as now Maddi was beginning to realize) it ought to be a reflection of who we are and who we aspire to be, on a multitude of issues. And now that she was beginning to realize just how insignificant we all are as individuals, to turn over all of our public involvement to one winning candidate for all the public concerns that representative will inevitably have to command, is certainly an archaic and intellectually debilitating way to run one's life. It is a method and a mechanism encouraging laziness, or worse apathy and stupidity, not to mention that through its very operation, it does silently (but deliberately) create and fosters the hidden agenda of betrayal to become the predominant cache of politics. Creating a false sense of maintenance in all things (at least for the period between elections), as deception and camouflage now becomes a top priority, which in a responsible world of public affairs, shouldn't exist. "Keep 'em happy and keep 'em stupid," becomes part of machinery that is itself counter-productive to a system that is supposed to be about "We the People." Therefore, any candidate who lobbies that they're the man (or woman) for the job, who doesn't have a comprehensive plan for electoral reform as the primary purpose for their being elected, such an omission should tell us immediately that they (or that person) are either too naïve for the job that they are undertaking, or that they know exactly what they're doing and that (as aspiring managers only, as opposed to being true leaders) they plan to betray us on a number of issues right from the start.

So it occurred to Maddi that so powerful is the rhetoric around our system that any real candidates who just want to question how things get done, in the hopes that they might actually try to fix things, really just can't: because their efforts to do so are just too easily twisted by the establishment (and the unthinking) into being something that is un-American. From a personal perspective Maddi had seen such reactions herself numerous times; when as a teenager, she had witnessed her mom's and dad's friends respond to Robert's rants on holiday occasions where at the dinner table if Robert tried to make one of his points, everyone would just go silent because each of them seemed to be subconsciously aware that if they engaged the conversation, that either their opinions would be exposed as owing too much allegiance to, too rigid a preset of social dogma, such as adhering to a particular party affiliation; or that their opinions would show too much (unthinking) deference towards the current dictates of the existing constitution. Or, worse (for them) if they expressed their opinion as an inquiry; that they run the risk of appearing passive and ill-informed, leaving themselves open to condescension of some "blow hard," who in such situations, typically tries to dominate such conversations with the correctness of their own views. Either way in a polite setting, where most have already succumbed to some (systemic) predisposition already on public issues, that everyone knows that any counter views will eventually lead to an uncomfortable standoff, where either feelings will be hurt, or an unpleasant confrontation will arise. So everyone knowing the inevitable destination of almost every conversation about politics and public affairs, at a polite holiday dinner table, all seem to also silently agree to wait for the equally inevitable uncomfortable pause, knowing that then someone would then dutifully interject with an equally awkward joke for the purposes of breaking the tension and changing the subject back into something more palatable inside the second dimension. Such is the psychology of polite conversation; and so too, is this part of the machinery that encourages the apolitical to stay on the sidelines and become inevitably the mass betrayed, silent majority.

And this of course brought Maddi back to her own suspicions earlier as to how exactly, American democratically elected representatives, actually get their work done. Now of course she was very mindful of what Patrick had successfully explained earlier, and by explaining the three dimensions, such an explanation certainly demonstrated and revealed just how those who might be of a mind to, could choose to use what they know about us (such as our natural tendency to preoccupy ourselves with our first two dimensions) using such knowledge not for us, but against us; and from that she now understood why things didn't seem to work so well, because the very trust that the masses are told to believe in, cannot be relied upon at all. But this left Maddi with the obvious question, if our politicians are passing laws that are so self-serving, preferential and oppressive to the American constituency at large, how exactly (legislatively) does this actually get done? If the Republicans are doing it, where are the Democrats in their opposition? And if the Democrats are doing it, where are the Republicans? Isn't this why we have (at least) a two Party system to begin with, so that there is always an opposition to keep the other side in check?

Well to this Robert explained to Maddi on a particularly cold Saturday, that there are of course numerous ways to get controversial and preferential legislation passed. And naturally the number of ways increases with the level of sophistication, money and effort that is used to get it done; but as bad as this realization is; the truth is that since the representative system is founded on trust, the typically more aggressive forms of corruption (although still frequently used) such as bribery, black mail and violent intimidation, under the representative system such extreme measures are simply frequently not necessary at all. Why, because the law making system that has been adopted here in the US and in the west generally (the very way in which laws get passed); makes the simple vice of betrayal alone, sufficient enough means (in most cases) to give the rich and powerful exactly whatever it is they want.

As examples, Robert then demonstrated that there are three typical methods used by the rich and powerful to get what they want contrary to the interests of the general public; ... by simply relying on the misguided trust of the general public. The most straightforward way is to simply recognize that laws (especially those that have hidden agendas) are rarely simple things written and passed with two or three sentences. Usually the most diabolical laws are the longest ones, where a law purports to be one thing to the general public, with its stated purpose to be laid out in its title and in the first few pages; and then is to be later undone through its exceptions as laid out (for example) on page say: 56, section 12, subsection 6, paragraph 2, subparagraph iv. That's where the bill is undone. But where the bill needs to be completely reversed however, in order to favor some special group or industry, well those reversals that are the complete opposite of the initial purpose set out in the first few pages, are then laid out yet again on another subsequent page of, say: 73, section 4, subsection 2, paragraph 7, subparagraph ii.; of that very same bill. Or if that too, is still too readily noticeable, then the reversal can be buried in some other separate (but related) piece of legislation passed at some other time altogether. That's why lobby groups and committee hearings and subcommittee hearings are all so important to lobbyists, … those exercises are to ensure that everything gets done just right, … that is, just right for them. Ergo, the old adage: … the devil is in the details.

Another means by which preferential legislation gets past in the United States is through the passing of omnibus bills. These are bills that have a vast array of sometimes completely disassociated pieces of legislation on any number of unrelated issues that are all thrown together in a single bill so that the entire array is passed by a single vote in both the House and the Senate. Such "kitchen sink" legislation is more arduous to comb through and therefore things can be made more difficult to find if a particular interest group wants to avoid public scrutiny. And finally the other way preferential legislation gets passed is because either the Democrat or Republican 'whip,' simply instructs (behind closed doors) that the party on mass is going to support a particular bill (and at this point Robert leaned back in his chair and put on his best southern drawl accent, making it appear as if he had been practicing for this precise moment forever) and laments: "Ah hell Maddi, it's so well known that the politicians don't even read the laws they're passing these days ... that in Washington it's all about just raising money for them and whomever, that even those troublesome 60 Minutes guys and gals have gone and reported on it." Now if that wasn't enough, Patrick who has been sitting quietly up to this point can no longer contain himself and now has to throw in his pet peeve; and that is that where the purpose of the legislation is to create some sort of regulatory supervision for something of public concern, then the requirements for that particular person or industry can be established by creating acceptable "industry standards" that the industries then lobby (behind the scenes) to set up those standards for themselves. That's why one always hears on the six o'clock news or on CNN or any other network some spokesperson claiming in the defense of their client or company, that their actions were well within "industry standards" and/or "guidelines" because that should suggest that their actions were appropriate and legal. When in fact, those standards were complete "bullocks" from the start (as Patrick was apt to say on such matters) and entirely inadequate to the task at hand. The creation of industry standards therefore is frequently just another self-legitimating diversionary ploy, the authenticity of which (if they are to be challenged at all), is to be dealt with (conveniently) on another day. And what the public rarely realizes is that this is how in fact a guilty bad apple within an industry then causes the more legitimate players in an industry to come indirectly (and even sometimes regrettably) to the aid of the guilty party, because any change in industry standards will then affect them, as well. And the question then becomes, that once caught in the act, ... what (if anything) will then any given industry do to one of its own. Or worse still, will an industry as a whole use those who get caught as a scape goat to mask what they as a group have been doing on a larger scale. Either way, through protection or through vilifying one of its own, the wealthy will re-establish the age old dichotomy of politicians and industry leaders being at odds with the needs of the general public; thereby reinstating the recurring paradigm of "us vs. them."

A recent example of this "us vs. them" paradigm, is currently taking place at one of its most horrendous extremes is the recent (and not so recent) water purification crisis occurring for the past few years in Flint, Michigan. In Flint due to cost restraints, and the city's own receivership issues, the City of Flint changed its water supply from Lake Huron and the Detroit River to the Flint River which had pipes that used fewer corrosive metal inhibitors, thereby these less protected pipes caused increased and unsafe lead contaminants to be included in Flint's water supply. This decision then caused a measurable spike in the blood-lead levels of its inhabitants most noticeably in the children which (when exposed to any increased toxicity levels of lead) is known to directly impair brain development and result in measurably decreased future cognitive abilities. When Flint city inhabitants complained that their water was discolored and tasted poorly and when people were forced to go to the hospital for testing and treatment; although action from local, state and federal authorities was to follow; one public comment stated that in the meantime, if there was any damage done to the children, it should only amount to the loss of "a few IQ points." Once again, reaffirming the long-standing and underlying expendability perspective, for the general public at large.

It Doesn't Have To Be This Way.

So the historical trends that had caught Robert's eye both as a student and later as an academic, was that as time changed, as supposedly advances and historical abuses of the past were stopped or even corrected; the dichotomy of "us vs. them" did not change. What was visible to Robert (and anyone else who cared to look) was that as society became (slowly) more enlightened over the centuries and as greater literacy and new technologies made their impact on our physical world, so too did the privileged adapt their approach as to how they would continue to differentiate themselves from the masses. Originally, when societal stratification was far more primitive than it is now, brute force and the corresponding power to dictate on supposedly enlightened matters entitled the presumed elite to arrogantly profess their superiority through falsified theories of superior breeding and proven bloodlines, enlightened cultures as opposed to those which were deemed to be "pagan," as opposed to the equally ridiculous pretense of dehumanizing a particular race or culture due to visibly different physical characteristics. Such false intellectual rationalizations may have been sufficient (with the aid of the whip and chain) to suppress the multitude during more primitive times, but with the changing of times these more overt and crude methods of oppression could not maintain themselves even from within their own ranks, because although such high societies were premised on the vices that represent the worst of us (vanity, arrogance, snobbery, ego, etc.), even the elite had amongst themselves those who, through their own logic and reason, were compelled to recognize and denounce the internal hypocrisy of their own self-serving agendas.

And even though it may be that the human traits of kindness, mercy, and generosity proved to be even more powerful than the self-serving vices of separation; regardless of the cause, as each false theoretical premise fell, and the more overt methods of oppression (like slavery) were dispensed with; the question as to what was to follow, was not the fact that the rich and powerful had finally and uniformly seen the error of their ways, but rather for those who chose not to evolve, the question for them became: what new form of exploitation was to take its place.

So from the time of the sealing of the Magna Carta to the signing of the Declaration of Independence, as the privileged used the theory of liberty to harness the enthusiasm of the masses for appeasing them with the promises and hopes that the lowest of them might someday see change for themselves; so too did the elite in manipulating such enthusiasm, succeed in maintaining their own privileged position, harnessing the strength and the needs of the of the masses for the promotion of their own self-serving ends by employing an ever more sophisticated means of deceit and betrayal. So as unrepresentative aristocracies were to originally play upon the folklore of an accountable Parliament for the furtherance of their own prestige; and an Imperial British Parliament was to later exploit the unrepresented colonies; and our Forefathers during their demands for equality were to abandon the slaves, all women and the property less; and the Civil War amendments were to be abandoned for institutionalized segregation; and the industrial revolution was to prey upon the immigrant and urban poor; what became less and less necessary was any need to engage in any of the old more overt forms of oppression. What was more efficient, were the more covert applications of deceit and betrayal, which effectively put the interests of the wealthy well ahead of everyone else. Therefore, in the more enlightened (postindustrial) times where tangible material wealth meant far more than "titled" class stratification. The eventual rise of mercantile, and later industrial commerce; far outpaced any previously obtained advancement in agrarian wealth; so much so that it no longer made any sense for the West to continue to engage in any of the more archaic overt forms of oppression when modern day covert methods would be far less visible, less obvious and hypocritical, and therefore politically less controversial. So with the adoption of universal suffrage, the West was able to maintain its claim as the slow, but progressive champion of liberty while in the meantime it had replaced the previous mechanisms for mass overt exploitation, replacing it in favor of the less conspicuous oppression of simple supply side economics, as it was practiced through the modern day mechanism of industrial capitalism.

So although with the 20th century, universal suffrage became a reality, that achievement although trumpeted as a great achievement for the West was just a side show for the rich as now the much larger game of controlling industrial and technological industries were where the real separation of society, was to be. The truth was that by the end of the 19th century and the beginning of the 20th century, with the advancement of the industrial revolution; big money through the likes of the Barclays, Rothschild, Morgan Stanley, the Rockefellers, Andrew Carnegie, Hearst, etc., had already like never before, in the history of man, already secured their corporate strangle hold on our politicians and our political system so that opposing the vote in any official capacity would itself have been inevitably counterproductive to the larger corporate agenda. The rich and powerful in the West would now find it more useful to work behind the scenes through the legislative means of committees and subcommittees to give the appearance of being both a good corporate citizen, that had a nation's political blessing; rather than to be seen as working against the democratic myth. The closest comparison might be to compare the north's position to support the abolitionist movement in the years prior to the American Civil War, the north wasn't opposed to human exploitation, it was more opposed to slavery (with its whips and chains) that made human exploitation look bad. The industrial north before the war could afford to appear progressive because it did not need slaves due to its own unlimited supply of impoverished immigrant workers from Europe to provide the necessary cheap labor for its factories and sweatshops. Similarly, in the 20th century the corporate agenda had grown so great that it could easily tolerate the political movement towards an expanded vote.

The problem however politically with the (so called) achievement of universal suffrage, is that where a society wishes to maintain itself as a privileged based society, and yet through universal suffrage there are more populous groups clamoring to have access to the public purse, the successful politician (in order to get elected and thereby gain control over that public purse), must promise more things to more people creating a never ending expansion of the modern day social welfare state. But with the modern day differentiation of society being now based on the mass accumulation of asset and liquidity wealth (those being the physical things of assets and currency), there quickly becomes an automatic apparent shortage of wealth to go around. Why, because as there are more outstretched hands in need of wealth distribution and since it is contrary politics (in a democracy) to say "no" to the multitude in need; and yet the rich want to hoard what they can while paying as little as possible, an automatic conundrum results where if one side does not yield to the other, than the system runs the risk of exposing itself as being either a nonresponsive (elitist and phony) democracy, or an ever increasing egalitarian (or dare it be said, socialistic styled) democracy. And the problem with this irreconcilable dilemma is that the West has chosen almost uniformly to solve this problem, by choosing a solution that does not solve it at all. The solution in the West has been to provide for both by, engaging in the short-term solution of deficit spending.

With deficit spending each nation state is allowed to amass a debt (an overall yearly accumulation of national debt) that allows that nation to meet its fiscal (financial) responsibilities (and promises) for any given year (not indefinitely) but to a mathematical extreme. That mathematical limit is where the servicing of the accumulated debt is measured in contrast to that nations apparent ability (through its current taxing capabilities) to continue to service the interest payments on that debt. And the problem with this solution is that as the national debt rises from year to year, with each yearly deficit being added on to the last, the overall national debt increases correspondingly giving this short term budgetary solution a finite life span, where no more loans will be granted once the interest of the accumulated debt becomes more than the tax base can continue to pay. And herein lies the new form of servitude, because as each government borrows to pay its bills for each new year, the actual interest needed to pay for the growing accumulated debt goes up per year as well, and this increased cost must be paid out of the received tax revenue for the current year by the taxpayer. And this means that the current taxpayer is the ultimate loser, as each generation is put into an ever (worsening) regressive situation. Why, because from a purely mathematical perspective, as the interest charges on the accumulating debt must command an ever increasing bite out of the current tax revenues, this means that if the same governmental services and programs are to be maintained the yearly taxes of the tax base must go up simply because the yearly interest charges on the yearly increased debt has gone up. Or mathematically, if the tax revenues are not correspondingly increased than the services provided must be scaled back. So in either case the current taxpayer is either required to perpetually pay more, or perpetually receive less. But there is a further problem with this mathematical model, which is that in reality there is (because of corruption) a third (but more diabolical) alternative that can be taken, which if chosen however, is worse in consequence than the stated outcomes of either of the other two. And that choice is to make slowly and systematically everything about the state ... a substantive lie. The alternative here is that because a nation state such as the United States operates from a single treasury, instead of visibly cutting back or outright cancelling government programs and/or services in order to balance its budget, the government through our elected representatives, can short change the services and programs already in existence so that they simply become a shallow veneer of what they profess to be.

Our politicians can do this because of their control over the treasury, money that was once allocated to fulfill a previous commitment can be reallocated to other priorities because even

97

within already divided departmental pools, the funds are just that: funds in a larger reserve to be tapped from one year to the next, according to that year's particular priorities. Such a practice as this, means that a program can stay in place for the political purpose of claiming that the program still exists, but its funds to fulfill its purpose, will be less than what it was the year before, and probably even less again (each year) in the years to follow. And if enough time is allowed to pass, while this regressive (and exploitative) practice goes on unchecked, the end result of most of what the government claims to be … thus becomes a lie.

Now it may appear that such a practice like this can go on only for so long, moreover some may even argue that it is indeed appropriate that each year all politicians should review existing budgets to see if there are any cost cutting measures that can be taken; but although this may be true, there is a far more sinister tactic that is undeniably being utilized as well when this practice is being used; and that is that when a government sets up a program or service that in the end it knows it has underfunded and cannot fulfill its purpose (as in the case where someone who walks through an agency's door, only to be overwhelmed by line ups, red tape and bureaucratic administration so that by the time that the person in need extends themselves to secure whatever the agency is supposed to offer, only to find out that the service promised is not to be there; such a process as this, is itself diabolical because this very result was possibly not only anticipated (but even hoped for) because it separates such individuals in need into at least two separate (political) groups. The first of these individuals are those who become defeated and ultimately accept their marginalization and abandonment as a way of life, and the second are those who actually get something for their application (but not what they actually need) and because they walk away with something less, but at least something; any protest that follows (during hard times) will lack any significant clout because they at least got something. In either case however a political benefit comes to those who did indeed short change the program, in that politically both the defeated and the disappointed become effectively neutralized as citizens with a legitimate grievance. Why, because either they've accepted their loss and being so demoralized and defeated they just move on empty handed, which is the plight of most of America's homeless; or as with the devastated group, they become so embittered (because they feel cheated) that they are no longer willing to work within the system, and should someone try to reach out to them, their anger and frustration effectively alienates most, if not all, of those who (in the absence of such hostility) might otherwise have taken up their cause.

And although this scenario of disengagement (through deceptive cutbacks) appears to be a problem for the poor and the working poor, what most Americans need to realize is that this scenario of government by frustration and ineffectiveness has a multitude of devastating consequences. Such hardships that (not so long ago/ pre 2008) were thought to be more the exclusive reserve of the poor, are now really more mainstream, as the middle class has now slipped in its financial prowess after the fall of 08. What this means is that the middle class and the lower middle class have lost their voice in American society. Why, because having been through the experience of already standing in such lines, having already had the experience of losing their job, or being stripped of their life's savings or suffered through a home foreclosure;

because of the not so distant events of 08, now more Americans live in fear, causing them to take on a more besieged mentality as a form of coping with (as opposed to pursuing) the rest of their lives. Why, because they know (that through no fault of their own), that they could once again be in that unemployment line, or in need of food stamps, or in need of a bankruptcy consultant, should surprisingly once more (through some allegedly "unavoidable" event) hard times should strike yet again. And the collateral consequences that come with increased poverty (or even the mere threat of poverty) is anger, and with anger comes impatience and intolerance, because in a western society everyone knows (especially here in the USA), that should you lose everything that you have, that such losses carry with it the stigma of failure and blame, regardless of the fact that what you had (such as a job) was surreptitiously taken from you. Not surprisingly, therefore such despair and anger then breeds hostility that has no otherwise identifiable cause but to sense (if not to fully understand) the betrayal that is attached to a distant and behemoth government that (just eight years ago) watched while the middle class and the lower middle class crumbled, but still found a way to harbor and look after the wealthy. The true consequence of the recession of 08 is that the rich are now astronomically richer than they were ever before, and the middle class and expanding lower middle class, now know that they are but one mere step away from absolute poverty. ... And yet the pundits in the mass media every night fain astonishment at the rise of a political outsider such as Donald Trump. Like it or not, since it has only been eight years, Trump has reactivated the disengaged, and somehow yet each network on the nightly news ... with their political commentaries, all seem so astonishingly surprised?

These are the by-products of not only a failed political economy but they are also the by-products of a society that is itself in a narrow pursuit of (perceived) freedom. It is a failed political economy because during better times, our politicians fail to search for alternatives to fix what is truly wrong. In our (too often) two-dimensional pursuit to enjoy our own lives, and better ourselves; we also fail ourselves during the good times, because that's when we know that those in power use their understanding of our third dimension (that part of us that relies on our so called representatives to protect our public affairs); that they deliberately use our reliance on them, to 'use what they know about us, not for us, but against us;' because they not only ignore what is wrong during the good times, but they also steal from our minimalist infrastructure, so that when difficult times do emerge, much of what we thought we had in place, … exists in name only. FEMA, with its unfinished (not to mention its preferential) business in New Orleans from 2005; and its additional failures on the Jersey shores from 2012, are a case in point. And worse than the failures of FEMA in both of these disaster zones was the lack of federal oversight that abandoned the claimants as they then again fell victim to the absolute attempts at fraud on the part of the insurance industry to deny the claimants within these disaster relief zones (after home owners lost everything) of the paying out their rightful claims.

At this point, Patrick again can no longer contain himself and he interjects to emphasize that the biggest problem not only in the United States, but with western democracy generally, is that once in power no one in power now actually tries to really fix anything. Not even the things that are broken that are supposed to be most sacred. And the reason for this is that, when it comes to reforming anything, it is less conspicuous (and therefore more politically advantageous) to bleed something to death then it is to kill it outright. Because, to close down an agency or a program, one makes enemies; but if you bleed something to death, by absconding its funds, the fatal wound is hidden in the budget, … and yet somehow new money (per se') surprisingly becomes available to make (or buy) new friends for the moment. Pre-existing infrastructure therefore, is one of the most powerful impediments to a healthy change in government (actually making change) because not only does a new politician not want to make new enemies, but government contracts are frequently large and lucrative and already exist as the bastion of the rich and powerful. So real change in policy and programs don't frequently occur; why, because most often the wealthy contractors simply don't want the change to begin with.

Now excitedly, Patrick points out that doesn't mean however that change is impossible when the situation becomes dire enough. For example, in Canada there is currently an exciting new Prime Minister who has acknowledged that frequently maintaining the status quo in any government portfolio for too long can, not only become part of the problem, but be catastrophic as well. In this regard, Canada's universal health care system is in financial crisis because the health care costs have been spiraling, not only year after year, but compounded with each passing decade as well; so in a radically bold move Canada's Prime Minister is floating a revolutionary solution to the problem by suggesting that an alternative hospital structure be created and phased in, where community based hospitals would be future funded by the proceeds raised privately through a correspondingly locally based, locally run, lottery. Now hospital lotteries themselves are not a new idea, but the complete funding of an entire hospital through a single weekly or monthly lottery is revolutionary. And in order to ensure that the vast amounts of necessary funds are raised, both the federal and provincial (state) levels of government are prepared to step aside and make all purchases of those particular hospital's lottery tickets, completely tax deductible. This means that each city population can fund free health care directly for themselves with new revenues, without any increased taxes or insurance fees; knowing all the while that their money is going directly to their local hospital and not into the government treasury where it can otherwise be misappropriated. And the automatic tax deduction that comes with each losing ticket, while having a measurable impact on the federal treasury, will be more than offset by the reduced governmental expenditure of the government trying to run a universally free health care system itself. It's a win/win, no lose situation, because either the idea will only partially work, and the hospitals will still require some government assistance, but not nearly what they currently require; or the idea will be a block buster success and the hospitals will run the risk that they will make too much money, and the government will have to apply the brakes and limit, in the future, the amount of tickets that can be purchased with a tax deductible benefit. Either way, the people of Canada are the big winners as they self- fund their own free and universal health care system not only immediately, but for decades to come.

Now, why is this idea important to us here in the United States, its important because just as universal health care is a "sacred cow" in Canada, the same untouchable stature (supposedly) exists here in the United States for our Armed Services and for those who have served and who are now in need of adequate funding for their care through our VA (Veteran Affairs) hospitals. You see, we could use the same plans as being discussed in Canada for our veterans, we could ask the President to work with each of the individual states, and to have an agreement that each state or city create a lottery based VA hospital where the tickets purchased would be tax deductible at either the federal or state level of government, so that within each state there would be at least one fully funded VA hospital with all the bells and whistles for our wounded veterans. Just imagine the type of money that could be raised, if in all of the fifty states there was a Powerball type lottery for Veteran's hospitals where in each state, the tickets themselves (as losing tickets) were all tax deductible. And as for the possibility of corruption seeping in, what the Canadians are mulling over is that the finances of the hospital be run by a Board of Directors of elected volunteers from each city and community, so that the finances are locally managed with no conflicts of interest, so that it becomes the highest compliment of your community (and a most sacred trust) to even be asked to run as a possible Board member (unpaid volunteer) overseeing the operations and fiscal management of your local VA hospital. ... And you see, this is the type of thing that can be done when politicians agree to step aside and stop padding the pockets of their friends and contributors with fat, juicy public contracts. And any excuse as to why this sort of initiative hasn't happened already, is because sadly ... we, the masses, truly are (in their eyes of those who are in control) all expendable, and yes, this applies even to all of our veterans; and all the excuses for not doing something like this so far, are absolute lies, ... or as Patrick likes to say ... pure "bullocks".

So How Bad Is It For The Millennial's?

So what's wrong with America? It's the concept (held by some, the establishment) that the majority of Americans (as individuals) are expendable. Now as we have seen this is not something that is new to America, Great Britain or even the west generally, it's just due to the fact that when America was first settled by our European ancestors they had a fresh opportunity to make a choice, but so intoxicated however did they become with the potential wealth that lay before them in the frontier, that in making the choices that they did, they allowed the worst within themselves, and the worst of themselves, to take America down a path of maximizing prosperity at the expense, and through the exploitation of others. You see, it is unclear however, how predisposed the first American colonists were to becoming the worst of themselves, or not. Clearly, indentured servants, and slaves already existed in Europe, but the question of whether or not that practice was to be adopted (on mass) with the colonists in the new world was not necessarily a forgone conclusion. During these early times much of the economy was based on self-subsistence and trade, so opportunities for mass exploitation were not a societal issue. Isolated incidents of exploitation did however exist such that when the first abducted slaves arrived from Africa they were treated as other indentured servants who could acquire freedom after years of forced servitude. So although the seed for old world human corruption was brought over with the original settlers, it didn't necessarily have to be planted, and even the acceptance of indentured servants didn't mean that the colonists to the new world had to adopt the evil practices of slavery. However, with establishment of settlements came power, and once the established colonists had taken root, that once the immense profits from such things as the tobacco fields became the "apple" of their eye; the colonists surrendered to being the worst of themselves and by 1641 slavery was officially legalized and established in the Massachusetts Bay colony. And so with establishment, came increased power, and with established power, the better part of humanity, became (like the plight of the Native American) an original American casualty.

From that point forward greed and the selfish need for cheap labor allowed the established in the 16 and 1700's to prosper. Because of a wealth in natural resources and land, those who became established needed cheap labor to continue to prosper and where possible to expand where they could. The cotton gin of 1794 allowed the labor intensive harvest of cotton to expand rapidly inland from the southern coast because with that mechanism the seeds of a heartier strain of cotton, that grew inland only, such seeds could now more rapidly be removed to increase harvesting yields. So with respect to the new world, from the earliest of times, two clear trends then started to emerge in the 16, 17 and 1800's. The first was that the prosperity of those who were in a position to prosper most, could maximize their profits best, where they could exploit their labor force the most. So in the agrarian industries, slavery clearly maximized the profits of the plantation owners to the extreme. And in other industries too, where labor was absolutely critical but slavery was ill suited, and where wages had to be paid; a maximization of prosperity for the industrial owners was realized when adequate wages were denied. So wealth maximization through exploitation of others, was an initial trend within the American economy, almost from the very beginning. And because of the frontier that was available, for four straight centuries the need for increased labor therefore was also continuously in demand. From the agrarian needs that dominated the 16 and 1700's to the industrial needs of the 1800's to the cattle and steel needs of the late 1800's, to the munitions needs of the early 1900's, to the automobile, appliance and technology needs of the late 1900's; in all four centuries with few exceptions (such as the Great Depression of the 1930's) there was a constant demand for cheap labor. So where the first trend was to exploit labor to maximize profits and through the retention of those profits in order to maximize the material separation of class and condition between the established elite and the masses, the second trend was that real economic and material growth was also being realized for the economy itself in all of America's four previous centuries. So, through labor, and with the abundance of natural resources made available through an expanding frontier, America's economy grew into the only economic industrial super power of its time, despite the growing disparity of wealth that was also rapidly taking place between the classes, at the behest of the rich and powerful. And the modern America that we know today, came about after the Second World War because of the domestic expansion in homes, trains, military equipment, ships, cars, roads, bridges, skyscrapers, planes, airports, schools, hospitals, hotels, utilities and power plants, telecommunications, industrial tools, farm equipment, appliances, furniture, clothing, shoes, ... all these things and so much more, were built here, in America with American labor. And through the use of the American workforce (although outrageous in who it abandoned and left behind), the second trend of achieving real growth continued, because American industry generated enough immense growth in wealth that despite the profiteering and gouging of corporate America, there was growth enough to see at least some wealth trickle down to the working classes. Thus, for the four centuries before the 21st, there was created therefore, slowly, a very real middle, and lower (working) middle class, for America; not because it was the goal of the rich to do so, but rather because of the immense enormity of what was actually being built in America.

Such is not to be the case however in the 21st century version of the global economy. Corporate America and America's elite can now maintain their profits (including their disproportion acquisition of world wealth) while sending whatever employment attached to their industries to other more favorable labor markets. The procurement of a global economy gives our industrialists access to labor markets in the form of out sourcing like never before. Telecommunications and international shipping lanes make possible, that all manufactured goods (that were once made in America) can be made elsewhere, where the poor will work for less, not for the purpose of hopefully becoming more active consumers themselves within their own nations (although that might be the working poor's fanciful dream); but more realistically, they'll do it, just to survive.

And it gets worse, the rich and the powerful of the world no-longer really adhere to one nationality, the wealthiest of the wealthy are welcome in almost all nations in the hopes that should they touch down for any length of time within any nation state it is hoped by those that receive them, that such a stay may cause the wealthy to set up shop and leave some of their wealth behind. The problem with this scenario is that because each nation is in competition with almost every other nation, there is now frequently a race to the bottom to not only impose as few restrictions as possible on global corporations, but a burden to even subsidize (at a nation's expense) the recruitment of such corporate giants. So this creates a multitude of problems for the foreseeable future, first the original concept of any sort of corporate national allegiance can no longer be counted on in any way whatsoever, and any nation state's suggestion that a corporation isn't completely free to do as it pleases with its resources, is apt to initiate a corporation's desire to take up residence elsewhere, or conversely is likely to dissuade any outside corporation to even consider setting up shop (within any given nation's borders) in the first place. Thus the rulers of the world in this global economy are no longer the leaders of our nation states, but rather the CEO's of the biggest and most powerful corporations world-wide.

And on the issue of the cost of labor since the borders of the world for corporations seem to be disappearing, and yet as a source of labor the peoples of the old guard nation states are trapped within their nations through their citizenship, each population becomes pivoted against each other in a competitive race towards the bottom for the lowest wages. So the poorest of India have to compete with the likes of the wages in Indonesia, Vietnam and China; and possibly poorer than all the rest, is the logistics of the entire population within the continent of Africa. The point being that there is no shortage, for even possibly a century to come, for long term further global corporate access to available, impoverished and exploitable labor.

The consequence of this means that all or most of the worlds unskilled labor requirements that are transportable because they generate mass consumer products will seek out (or be drawn or driven to) those nations that have the most available and cheapest labor. This will create a shortage of such work in the developed (first world) nations such as here in the United States which means that all promising employment prospects in America and the west generally will be more of the higher end variety of skilled and trained labor. And this of course might be all well and good if there are accessible buyers for the higher end products to be delivered, but in a world where there is a race to the bottom in wages, the assumption that there will be a consumer class created sufficiently wealthy to buy the higher end products of the world where bare subsistence is still part of the developing world's daily routine, is itself an assumption that puts high tech industries at risk. This becomes especially so if the growth in those developing markets should become interrupted, or should slow down for some reason. The current concerns for the reliability of China's emerging and growing middle class is a case on point, because if China's growth in its middle class should slow or become stunted so that the masses who have emigrated from its rural regions to its urban centers should have a spike in their unemployment; where the young should be forced to go back and live a more simple (unemployed) rural existence with their parents, even for a short period of time, such a change in circumstance (if large enough) could have an extreme chilling effect on a consumer market which will then spill over as a slowdown in high end industries worldwide.

On top of this, there are also other concerns attached to the US not having enough manual labor jobs available for its own populous and that is that as more individuals are abandoned by an economy that emphasizes job prospects only at the mid-range to higher end of employment spectrum, those who miss that particular escalator are more likely to be in need of government assistance in the form of social assistance just in order to survive and this of course will only create a greater tax burden on those who are gainfully employed. And as the tax demands rise, that means that there is less disposable income for the employed, and then this too will have its own immediate ripple effect on our domestic economy as well. The United States is based on a consumer economy, so at some point in the absence of vigorous wage increases, between the high turnover rate of gadgets that we are supposed to consume, with their hidden user fees, surcharges, etc.; and the additional consumer (or what is called consumption) taxes that are being increasingly imposed; between all of these costs and expenditures it is only a matter of time before the typical US consumer is tapped out. Proof that this might already be happening is the current trend now taking place in the auto industry, where in order to keep the volume of car and truck sales at near record highs, options to finance vehicles for lengthier periods of time up to eight years; with little or no trade in requirements are now being offered. Such prolonged financing packages are worrisome, because they can be representative of an otherwise soft market for sales of what is characteristically known as a big ticket (consumer purchase) items. The question is, is the need to offer such generous financing indicative of a trend that wages have not kept up to the higher end products that America has slowly but increasingly become reliant upon, or is it the first signal that the employment claims of our prognosticators are not as robust, or as stable, as they have lead us to believe. Could it be that the fears of those who were hurt most in 08, might be themselves a more reliable barometer for where we are now in our economy (and have a better sense of what lies beyond the visible horizon) than do our so-called experts. It may be old fashioned, but certain individuals just seem to know that a storm is coming just because their ailing arthritic joints (or migraine sinuses) tell them so. And in our world where our media (because they too are undeniably big business) are themselves adverse to talking about systemic corporate exploitation; that they, in pulling their punches, may leave us in a position of uncertainty. Maybe, those who suffered the worst economic injuries of 08, are this time around (as they see big business once again engaging in generous financial packages) are themselves, in a corrupt world, with their reluctance to jump at what they know they might not be able to maintain, are now our most reliable economic forecasters?

The Sum Total Of The Conversation From Hell

So as each semester starts to come to a close, in each of his classes in both business law and political science, Robert starts to try to sum up and bring together the intersecting and contributing themes of both politics and business in trying to explain where America and the millennial students find themselves today. This is the message that earlier Robert professed that he, and so many others, seemed to miss. It is the message that even if Robert hasn't got it entirely right on everything, the message is that all the various topics that have been discussed in his classes that these issues are all (in an overall pursuit of the truth) indeed connected. It is the exact message that history is constantly repeating itself precisely because we are in denial, we consistently treat all of these supposedly disconnected topics as if they are not only unrelated, but also because we are conned into believing that the things that caused the wrongs of our past, are now behind us. The con is to give us examples of periodic accomplishments (like the occasional winning hand) so that we see the western representative state as a mechanism of progress and advancement, instead of a device that time and again brings its contempt for its constituency to a point of boil, only to then grant some sort of victory only (to keep us at the table) so that the more methodical forms of harsh and prolonged oppression can continue. The propaganda is to focus on the moments of achievement instead of the centuries of the many millions who had to endure abuse, torture and murder while a select minority few took privilege and separation from a representative system that served them best. The prevailing propaganda would tell us that the recent decades of disproportionate shootings of young black males in their communities such as Chicago or the current nationwide highly visible deaths of blacks by our law enforcement officials, are themselves matters that are not systemic, but rather societal failures that need to be addressed and worked out currently, through such things as progressive youth programs and better law enforcement screening and training protocols. Resistant would be all those in power who would deny that its America's institutional (hidden) agenda of betrayal to do as little as possible for as long as possible, that is actually to blame; in order to retard the social progress of America so as not to impede the existing benefits of the privileged few for as long as possible.

Included in this denial would also be the rejection that the continued deaths of individuals, by either community gang warfare or rogue police officers in the meantime, are not themselves just more expendable casualties, towards a larger hidden agenda of simply playing for time. This is the message that has been lost due to the deliberate distraction of the occasional periodic victory. The agenda of systemic delay is protected against criticism because such a criticism isn't against necessarily something tangible, but rather is a criticism that enough isn't being done, and so the "Catch 22" begins all over again as the oppressed are asked once again to trust the very system that has betrayed them for centuries. The story is that there is no need for another Philadelphia Convention because a promise of "Real Change" this time, is to come with the next election.

And so in order to make this point, and in order to emphasize the message in the few remaining classes of each semester, is the recurring deceitful theme, that what's best for America, is that the masses are here to be subservient to the true agenda of what's best for the privileged few. And although, Robert believes that, despite the fact that this point should already be abundantly clear through the recognition of the fatalities described above; Robert feels further compelled to re-emphasize this reality in his closing classes, by focusing on America's current financial situation, which clearly demonstrates that even with the most rudimentary bookkeeping, one realizes (that with all of this in our past), ... America is now also running out of money.

That currently, America; even for a nation state as large as the United States, when you have such massive single expenditures as providing for a military and armed forces that are now expected to protect American interests all around the world, with America presently having military commitments in over eighty countries outside of its own borders it makes sense that with costs such as these, ... things would get expensive. But add to this responsibility, domestic expenditures such as any Medicare or Medicaid programs, a justice system, border patrol, homeland security, treasury, diplomatic services and embassies, foreign aid commitments, emergency services, disaster relief funds not to mention all other national agencies, programs, boards, departments, watchdog agencies, tribunals, federally assisted benefits, government youth programs, national parks and services, etc., ...remembering all the while that there are also to be added all the additional costs associated with providing for the US Congress, the US Supreme Court, and the Presidency as well, and the modern upkeep of all of the above. Consequently, with a spending ledger such as this, one would expect that money would be either tight, or even require government borrowing (as it does) just to pay its yearly bills. But when you add to these expenditures, and more; the funding (of interest) on an accumulated national debt that is now set to hit $20 trillion dollars by the year 2020 (if not sooner), it is not hard to see how a state of financial crisis is now at hand. And although up to recently, unlimited government borrowing has been the method used to keep the US

Government afloat, this too is now coming to an end as our debt to revenue ratio has come to near extremes, causing the global concern for US insolvency to become a discussion point, where more alarming to US lenders is the fact that should the US not reconcile its need for outside borrowing, that in order to fund itself it may have to reduce its deficit and the value of its overall debt by simply printing more American currency to make ends meet. This solution however, to those who lend America money is unacceptable. The printing of more money without outside restraint, means that a currency, any currency loses its buying power and that means that those who own US debt as an investment will lose on their investment even though the US is paying interest on that loan.

As a potential counter measure the IMF (International Monetary Fund) has increased its reserve fund of SDR's (Special Drawing Rights) which can be used in the future as an alternative potential currency between member nations allowing future loans to be borrowed and repaid in the same SDR's which, because they are held by the IMF, would prevent America or any nation from altering the value of a loan by simply printing more of their own money (because the extension of any future loans will be made in the form of SDR's). For the American people, this has large implications (although it is doubtful that we on mass will ever understand it until it's too late) first it means that the American dollar will probably stop being the world's reserve (most trusted) currency; and second it means that pursuing a rapid rate of growth with the assistance of a healthy dose of inflation in order to countermand and combat previous wage stagnation is unlikely. In this regard the public needs to realize that inflation is not necessarily a bad thing. In fact, sometimes vigorous inflation is absolutely necessary for an overall healthy (balanced) economy. What the public needs to understand is that the rate of inflation within the economy is like your heart rate within your body. Sometimes for overall health in order to keep our muscle mass healthy and strong we have to raise our heart rate to a vigorous rate for a short duration in order to increase (and even to maintain) current muscle mass and burn off fat. Similarly, the economy works in precisely the same way. Where our economy is our entire body, in order to feed and nurture our muscles (the people) we need a healthy blood flow, a healthy and robust exchange of flowing (liquidity) currency and an exchange of gases (oxygen and carbon dioxide / wages and goods and services). A vigorous heart rate brought about by increased activity is a good thing for the extremities of the body (such as the people) and it keeps our fat (our debt) in check. More oxygen equals healthier/ stronger muscles; more wages equals healthier/stronger people; ... you get the picture. But in making this analogy it is important to note that without strong (even robust) inflation, wage stagnation will weaken the people, (even from the start) although it takes time (like a lack of physical activity) to become noticeable. What the pundits always say is that a slow but steady inflationary rate of about 2-3% is best, and that would be true if that was to transcend equally and quickly down to wages as well, in a timely fashion; but what is more typical now (more than ever) since the 2008 crash, is that the grotesque hoarding of wealth by the rich and the powerful that occurred in the aftermath of 08, as (supposedly) our government tried to solve the problem, and head off a 1929 type depression; was that with that hoarding, the general public was to receive wage stagnation for the past eight years. This means that even at these conservative estimates our wages are at best already 16-24% behind. And this figure does not include the exceptional inflation that the rich have enjoyed and provided for themselves through their wage increases, as they have successfully widened the income gap between us and them. The point is that to them, it's a game of relativity. And worse still, is that instead of seeing our wages increase, the American people have been beaten psychologically so badly, that there is a silent majority among us that instead of pursuing their lifetime goals, they have silently become content (because they remember 08 so terribly well) just to keep their job. And as Patrick points out, you don't need chains if fear (any kind of fear/ this time economic fear) will keep the servants in line.

Now, at this point, it is important to pause and take a closer look at what happened in 08 if we are to understand its relevance on today's job market. Briefly what happened in 08 was this: Wall street had for decades been selling collateralized debt obligations (home mortgages) to the general public. These CDO's as they are called, were really just residential mortgages that were taken out by homeowners on their residential homes, but then sold to third parties as profit making instruments due to the interest that they were expected to earn. Now these (renamed) collateralized instruments were being sold by the banks to the general public as investments, because they were deemed to be so secure. What happened however was that over the years, as the number of available home mortgages (available for public sale) began to run out; Wall Street, in order to feed the appetite for these types of transactions, created subprime mortgages where someone could buy a house, and the lending institution in an increasingly competitive market, in order to get the mortgage, would offer in competition with other lending institutions (because there were not enough CDO's to go around, and yet Wall St. still wanted to maintain its commissions) encouraged a variety of interest rate inducements to be created, to maintain sales. For example, the first year or two of a subprime mortgage would have an extremely low rate, say 1% or even no interest at first (and that was the hook), but later it would by the terms of the mortgage, radically increase the rate from that 1% to 3 or 4% in year two, and to 8% in year three, and possibly so on after that. So the mortgage brokers and the realtors would aggressively push these mortgages on to the public for not only their personal homes, but also as second and third properties for investment purposes as well. So aggressive in fact, did this industry become, that the brokers started at first selling these homes and mortgages to retired people and individuals on fixed incomes, people they knew could never possibly pay the accelerated interest charges after the initial subprime (teaser) rate had expired; that later, they expanded the sale of these mortgages to include buyers who had neither assets, employment or income. It was all a big fraud, and the thinking was that as long as housing prices continued to rise; that provided that the subprime buyer flipped the house by selling it, before the teaser rate expired (or they could no longer afford the interest being charged), thereby discharging the mortgage, that everything would be fine.

Consequently, a false housing bubble was created, because the demand for housing that there appeared to be, was false. But the scale of this fraud was to go supernova in size, when the banks would routinely bundle up these subprime mortgages with other investments that weren't so sketchy, camouflaging the massive risk for default in these subprime investments, with other blue chip investments, and selling the bundle as if the entire bundle was a triple A secured investment throughout. And if that wasn't bad enough, the rating agencies such as Standard and Poor's or Moody's either knew, or turned a blind eye as to whether or not their rating of these investment products were as secure as their original triple A rating had claimed. The end result of this charade was that when the fixed income and no income buyers of the houses started to default on their accelerated mortgages in vast numbers, it came to-light that the bundled products that each bank was selling were not the secured investments that they claimed them to be, and this automatically caused a paralysis in sales and lending throughout the financial industry as no one knew or trusted what anything was really worth. The banks couldn't sell or loan to one another because it was unclear what they were selling or what they were using as collateral for many of their loans. Crisis had struck. What was to follow was that since the banks could not, or would not, lend to one another, the liquidity of the nation was at risk and the people who were in immediate jeopardy, as collateral damage were the smaller businesses that relied on a revolving source of credit to stay afloat, so a decision was made to enter into a policy of Quantitative Easing which was that the US Federal Reserve would advance billions to the banks in order that they could create new products for sale, and to loan (so as to prime the pump as it were), and this influx of lending ability would solve the pressing lack of liquidity problem. The solution meant that the banks would not have to absorb the losses; and the extension of the QE program for several years thereafter, beyond its original purpose, meant that billions became trillions of dollars, as these funds were made available to those who were in a position to take corporate advantage of this new money. That meant that the profits of the past were left mostly undisturbed and the profits from the new transactions were then to be tallied as new business. And the new money that went out to borrowers, because the lending world was now a much riskier place, that money was lent predominantly and preferentially to people and companies who already had strong assets to offset any risk that might be associated with the new loans, allowing the wealthy to benefit disproportionately from the stimulus, ...than the average American.

With the crisis of 08, and with the events that have followed since, the current economic situation therefore has changed dramatically for everyone. The jobs that have been created by virtue of Quantitative Easing are based on a flawed and inescapable theory of trickledown economics. Basically, the theory is that jobs are to be created by QE reserves as the borrowers predominantly purchase stocks (and bonds) on the financial markets. And although this may create wealth for some, it does not mean that it will create jobs. Why, because as newly created bank reserves do mean that there is (new or more) money to be lent to qualified borrowers, (aka the already wealthy, with existing assets) to buy more assets and stocks, such purchases do not necessarily mean that the company is going to create a representative amount of new jobs with those purchases. The company in receipt of the new loan has numerous choices at its disposal, it can either make a new acquisition (like buy another office tower already in existence) or it can buy more (paper) stock in another company; either way no measurable new jobs are created on the street, but the company's stock price goes up significantly because it now has more assets within its portfolio. This helps the already rich, because it is presumed currently that less than 10% of the population already owns as much as 40% of the stock market. Therefore, for an appreciable measure of job creation to take place, the rich would have to make job creation as one of their top priorities in choosing to take out the loan to begin with, and once the Quantitative Easing is turned off; there is nothing to compel (even the well intentioned borrower) to keep those jobs up and running. This is why the media and the pundits can claim that there has been in fact an economic recovery, but at the same time show slow and anemic job growth. Because it was a recovery for the already rich (and a few others), but not for the unemployed, or the newly unemployed, or the under employed, or the soon to be unemployed.

At this point Patrick pipes up and observes: Isn't it funny how selective the term "recovery" is, it's like "We the people" all over again. A "recovery" for who ... oh yes, those (special) "people." Ah isn't it all just so grand, that the deceptions of old, that were just recently thought to be of such a bygone era, are suddenly ... new again.

But unfortunately there's more. Not only are the job prospects to be scant and less reliable in the turn of millennium, but our ability to pursue our own hopes and dreams are now to be restricted as well. How, because there are new shackles to be imposed on the masses limiting our financial freedom (and consequently our broader pursuit of freedom generally) as a direct result of the catastrophe of 08 and the steps that were taken thereafter. What occurred, as a direct spin off of the Quantitative Easing solution is the realization that the process of Quantitative Easing itself is not without its limits. What Quantitative Easing does, is that it supposedly floods any domestic economy with new (liquidity) money which in turn is supposed to stimulate an economy so that once restarted, it can run (somewhat) on its own. Basically, the idea is that an injection of more money leads to more spending, more spending leads to more consumption, more consumption leads to more manufacturing, more manufacturing (in all things) leads to the need for more investment and borrowing, which leads to more jobs and employment, and this employment leads to more spending, but this time around, the healthier spending is based on growth, growth in current industries and growth in new industries; and although expanding industries and new industries may require more money, this time the injection of more money is healthier, because this time any borrowing that is made, is made in partnership with growing profits based on increased production.

Quantitative Easing by itself however, is expansion of the economy without (necessarily) production, and if an injection of quantitative easing doesn't create a cycle of production commensurate with the amount money injected, then the money injected (but not exercised or utilized for production), creates the economic equivalent of dormant economic fat. Ergo, the rich get immediately richer because, as we have already seen, what is standing in the direct path of this ideal, preventing it from becoming a healthy reality, is the direct obstacle of financial hoarding that takes place as the already wealthy get first (crack, as it were), access to this new money through financial institutions, such as the banks, and the bond and stock markets. Why, because the rich already have the existing wealth that puts the new money (which is a loan to begin with) at less risk; thereby creating the scenario, and the means, whereby the rich get richer, while the majority of the population, fall steadily behind. Inescapably therefore, quantitative easing as an economic stimulus theory only works, if the "trickle down" aspect of it, sees the new money not trickle down, but flow rapidly (in a high ratio/ to money loaned equation) into actual production (as opposed to the mere act of further asset acquisition). What the system then hopes for then is an inflationary trend that spans all aspects of the economy because as there is growth through demand of all things prices will naturally rise as each segment of the economic chain tries to realize for themselves a piece of the growth that is taking place. Put bluntly, the cost of raw materials will rise because the demand by refineries and smelters will increase, refined and processed materials will go up because there will be more demand placed on parts manufacturers, manufacturers prices will rise in order to meet larger demands of assembly plants, assembly plants prices will rise because there is an demand for new and innovative products, and new or improved products will see their prices rise because of the demand by consumers for their finished product. And all along the chain, because of a request for greater production more employees will be required and wages will be expected to rise because a valued work force will be necessary to keep production maximized at each segment of the chain; so too then will the available funds exist across a broader population for the consumption of all things, because the population will be financially healthy enough to buy new things.

Inflation therefore, is as much a critical component to a healthy economy, as is the need for a vigorous trickle down component of the available wealth. But this is not the situation that our financial establishment of the Federal Reserve, the Presidency and America's wealthiest have created, what the establishment has done is the they have created rapid inflation for themselves in the most expensive of things (such as luxury hotel rooms that cost over $20,000 a night) or where real assets experience strong inflation such as 10% or more per year for the best commercial real estate while at the lower end of the economic spectrum the debate seems to be whether to raise nationally, the minimum wage by as much as $2 dollars to a total of $12 dollars per hour. Or $15 dollars per hour, according to Senator Bernie Sanders. This is the situation that has been created where through the hoarding of available capital at the top, thus interfering with the downward cascade of wealth; and the devaluation of American labor through outsourcing to other nations who are just trying themselves to stave off desperation and starvation. The problem is that the American public generally doesn't know what's happening because it is not part of our daily routine to ask regularly (either monthly or even yearly); what the cost of the most expensive hotel rooms are, or to ask how many millions of dollars a fifty story Manhattan office tower is appreciating each year. Consequently, the system as a theory, and as a practical matter, has broken down entirely. And yet this is precisely the dilemma that we currently face, as we have now turned the corner and entered into the new millennium.

Where we stand today, is that since outsourcing of employment has already become a new and frequent reality, and certainly since the last two decades of the twentieth century it has been seen as a viable business practice to cut costs, outsourcing therefore (as a viable business practice) has only increased since the year 2000. But add to this, the financial hoarding that has taken place in the aftermath of 08, and what we see is the development of the exact opposite of a healthy economy; but rather, an economic regression where, yes: there is an increase in wealth accumulation for the preferred few, but also a much larger middle class regression as strong consistent employment has given way to more sporadic employment with fewer benefits, and wages have stagnated under the threat that to even request a raise, or to request anything more than a bare minimum raise of 1 or 2%, is met with the hostile (almost bull whip) reminder of how each sector is just on the verge of being outsourced entirely.

Thus the newest version of forced servitude gets its 21st century rebirth, because this time you can't leave (the casino) because the frontier is now fully occupied, and since the game you are being forced to play is called "your livelihood," if you step outside (like the gambler who goes out for a smoke), you thus now become unemployed; and once outside, there is no place to go.

So now in the new millennium where outsourcing is now part of our new domestic economy, so too has the solution of quantitative easing also become a potential threat in our new situation (because as a possible tool for the people) in that it has already been used to such an extreme to benefit the rich, that as a potential solution (in the foreseeable future) the practice of Quantitative Easing has already been exhausted and may not be available for us in the near future should another crisis arise. Why, because if used beyond a certain point, continued use of quantitative easing jeopardizes the value of a nation's currency because too much of a currency, disconnected from the economy that it fuels, becomes more and more just meaningless paper. So where quantitative easing has already occurred and has been taken to its mathematical extreme, then as a device it cannot be used again until sufficient growth has again been generated to allow for a further injection that will not put the currency at risk of being significantly devalued. This means that if quantitative easing has taken place and a significant amount has been hoarded through asset acquisition as opposed to healthy production, then the rich have not only ingratiated themselves with our nation's wealth, but they have also absconded with much of our nation's borrowing power as well. Because now, even if our national leaders should become so inclined to engage in another round of quantitative easing (but this time for the benefit of the middle and lower middle class), it could not do so without throwing the economy into a short bout of hyperinflation which, in order for that to be later restrained, our leaders would have to apply the brakes to the economy and of course this would then only hurt the middle and lower middle classes even more, as our nation would spiral into a violent recession with massive job losses being the first casualties.

So the end result of what has transpired to date is that through the policy of quantitative easing the US economy has supposedly expanded rapidly by (at least) the number of trillions that have been created through new bank reserves, and for those trillions that did not go into production but went into less productive things like asset acquisition, there has been significant inflation in the value of those assets such as office towers, mansions, hotels, stocks and yachts, because there was more money available to the wealthy, year after year (through more QE), to buy such things (for the rich) from one another. But now, that they the rich have already increased and inflated their own asset base, after quantitative easing has been brought to an end (because it has been taken to its mathematical extreme, and to do any more would be to start the US dollar down the road to becoming the economic equivalent of the Mexican peso) the problem now for the middle class and the lower middle class is that now the rich have so much, loans to the less affluent are already, and will increasingly become, more difficult to come by, for two primary reasons. First if you want to start a business from scratch, it will be extremely more expensive (should location be a factor) because there has already been robust inflation for prime real estate, in obtaining the optimum properties for manufacturing, commercial leasing or retail, to either lease or to own. So again, not surprisingly, the significantly wealthy get the best location for all things because they alone can afford it. And second, the middle class ability to borrow at all, has been significantly reduced because those who have money sufficient enough to lend (due to hoarding and their own asset appreciation) are now significantly less inclined to lend any necessary larger amounts to non-collateralized riskier new ventures, when they can lend that same money to those who are equally as rich as themselves, to reduce their own potential risk, or eliminate the possibility of risk altogether.

Thus, the chains of modern day servitude are brilliantly transformed into invisible restraints because the things that bind us now (in the new millennium) are not things at all, because today our chains are the things we don't have, such as a lack of borrowing power and a lack of liquidity that is available to the middle classes. This is why innovative shows, such as Shark Tank, are so very popular ... because they are in fact so very necessary; because the contestants no matter how ingenious their winning products may be, the winners needed to go on the show to secure from the ultra-rich the necessary capital for their product, because that capital was not available to them any other way.

So where in the 18th, 19th, and 20th centuries, the poor could escape the hardships that they faced by moving west into an expanding frontier, now that our frontier is exhausted, there is no place for the millennials to go. So whether the working class are limited just because they are just an "average Joe" (in a highly technical world), or the masses are limited by geography, or compromised by the fact that in any one place there are just too many of us, or because of the fact that we already lack money; the consequence of our new economy is that we will inevitably be denied the capital and liquidity for any potential basic startups, the very type of startups that are most likely to give us our best hope for the future. Why, because although there is significant and vast amounts of money through venture capital for the high-tech industries because they provide immense profits (sometimes 50-100% on the initial investment, or more) these are also the type of large scale manufacturing jobs that are more easily (through industry) eventually outsourced, and as for the high-end of engineering design areas of employment, such advanced jobs at present seem to benefit from being regionally concentrated to such specific technical regions as silicon valley. So broad based job creation through more typical startups such as restaurants, garages, local grocery stores, all sorts of retail shops, shoe repair, dry cleaners, retail clothing, local butchers, florists, bakeries and anything to do with small time manufacturing; the very sorts of enterprises that create healthy employment locally across the country will either have to go the way of the conglomerate chain, where minimum wage is all that can be hoped for, or cease to exist altogether because simple startups such as these can't get the basic capital to get off the ground. So by design, those who would have been slave owners in other times, are by their choices and actions of today (through their more sophisticated and invisible forms of oppression) have successfully transformed themselves, through their control over (and denial of) capital and liquidity, into ... the self-serving investment bankers of our time.

The Millennial's Solution: Tackling Hypocrisy Through Industry Sharing, Honesty and Integrity

Maddi had always loved real estate. The thought of owning her own house and making it a reflection of how she actually sees herself had always been a dream of hers. As she was growing up her vision of what she had envisioned was however, influenced if not dominated by what was around her, that being a more suburban perspective; but even as a teenager she realized that there seemed to be a big difference not only in suburban neighborhoods; but also, there was a big difference in quality and lifestyle from one street to the next even within the same neighborhood. But when she moved to New York City, that city took these differences to a whole new level. So the contrasts within New York City, not to mention the contrast between NYC and the rest of the country, would be a frequent topic of conversation between the three, as Patrick was now a permanent constant, on Maddi's weekend brunches with Robert.

And of course whenever you talk about real estate in New York City, the subject always ends up being about price. But what Madeline couldn't understand was that although the US had just gone through a housing crisis, where housing prices plummeted and at its apex Maddi remembers seeing perfectly good suburban homes being bull dozed to the ground on the six o'clock news; that as bad as that was, that the prices in New York City and particularly in Manhattan, had not only recovered since 2008, but Manhattan prices had now surged in price well beyond any of the other housing markets in the country. Now, when Maddi first asked her father why houses were being knocked down in 2010 to 2012, Michael explained to her that as things got worse, it got to the point where people actually owed more to the banks (on their mortgages) than the houses were worth; so the owners were simply walking away leaving the banks to foreclose and take ownership. And once a house was abandoned, not only did it continue to acquire expenses, such as unpaid property taxes, utilities, insurance and bylaw infractions, the exposure of un-kept and abandoned homes (on what were otherwise good streets), was destroying the property values of all the other homes on that street. Consequently, from one state to the next, different arrangements were made with local authorities to allow the banks to destroy the houses so as to stop both the amassing financial liabilities, but also to stop the depreciation contagion that risked the property values of so many other homes and neighborhoods.

In Manhattan however, the story was quite different. Since Manhattan was home to so many of America's wealthiest Americans, when certain of Manhattan's elite somehow suffered the same plight as so many other Americans by losing their jobs when they could least afford it; yes: those Manhattan homes and condos went on the market at drastically reduced rates, but because so many other residents of Manhattan were rich without debt, their houses were simply just taken off the market. These Manhattan homes and condos came off the market because the owners didn't have to sell. Only those who had to sell, sold their properties; but because the other prime properties around them were not going on the market (because of the sheer density of population and a continued demand to live in Manhattan) any perceived loss in market value, never actually became a loss because the other properties were never sold. And when the quantitative easing money did kick in, these people were the first to have their incomes restored, if not in fact enhanced as they took on new remuneration from the quantitative transactions. Consequently, the richest of Manhattan's elite (as a group) were able to prey upon the weakest of their own and pick up prime properties at a steal, while also being able to wait out the storm (as it were) until America's new expanded economy (based on quantitative numbers) gave Manhattan its own unique form of recovery. Ergo again, the already rich, simply got richer.

Now to Maddi, who had been brought up to think like her mother and father with a desire to make the world a better place for everyone, but also wanting to better her lot in life (because after all she was a business student) saw that maybe beneath the strong demand to live in Manhattan; that there might still be a business opportunity to be realized from all of the carnage of 08. So on one Saturday brunch, Maddi put to Robert the idea about creating a corporation that would buy properties, residential properties, where the newly created corporation and a young couple like Maddi and Patrick would buy a house or condo on a desirable street, … together. The objective would be that the corporation would go on title for half ownership of the property, and Maddi and Patrick would go on title for the other half, whereby Maddi and Patrick would move in thus becoming owner occupiers of the house, but only at half the cost. For the corporation the incentive would be that in exchange for paying half the asking price, Maddi and Patrick would agree upon any future sale of the house they would only take a maximum of 5% of the appreciation rate, per year (on their paid half) of the said house; and the corporation would be entitled to the rest of the accumulated appreciation. And in the meantime the house would be occupied and cared for by owners who would pay all of the taxes, maintenance fees and expenses, thus relieving the corporation of all continuing carrying costs on its long-term investment. To Robert this idea seemed fantastic, because this was a new approach to the purchasing of real estate that was consistent with what the millennials had already created for themselves through their attachment to Uber and Airbnb, and it was also consistent with the new millennial's overall (less selfish) "shared economy" perspective.

Obviously the market for this would be huge, because who wouldn't want to own a part of Manhattan, at half the price. Also the idea was brilliant from a corporate stand point, because not only would this type of corporation make Manhattan more affordable to everyone, thus creating even more demand for the hottest market in America; but for the purposes of long term pension plans in a world where now cash currency and sovereign debt are visibly suspect (if not completely vulnerable) to devaluation, it only makes good business sense as a pension plan for its managers to hedge the pension's financial (paper) assets with a strong bricks and mortar component within a broader diversified portfolio. Also the spin offs for such a corporation would be immense as the corporation could quickly expand into other extremely lucrative areas such as home renovations, and banking (because it would have an immediate client base, through the likes of Maddi and Patrick who could well be in need of both a renovator and a bank), plus the corporation could also branch out and become its own broker as a realtor, and it could even create its' own prepaid "waiting list" (a sort of front of the line benefit package) where those who are on the list, would have first access to some of the hottest real estate in New York City, … and again, all at half the price. And on the stock market as an IPO, such a corporation would naturally go through the roof, not to mention the fact that the concept could also be expanded to other hot American urban centers such as Miami, Seattle, San Francisco, and even Los Angeles (especially with that city's congestion problems) just to name a few. And of course there would be no reason for such a strategy not to flourish overseas to accommodate the likes of London, Paris, Berlin and Frankfurt.

For Robert this idea, as the days progressed began to demonstrate that it was more than just an intriguing new approach to real estate but was in fact representative of something more. Within this idea (and other ideas like it, such as Uber etc.) was a willingness to approach an industry from a more inclusive perspective where easier access to any given thing was approached from a shared rather than an exploitative perspective. Absent was the undercurrent historical trend towards separation, greed and oppression; and in their place was an honest and upfront request for corporate and political collaboration from surprisingly the very generation(s) that ought to be resentful (if not downright angry about the America that could have been), not to mention the anger that should have come from those had been denied so much (for centuries) all along the way. It was as if this idea (and the others like it) had the maturity to realize the futility in trying to change the way things are from within the established halls of power; that rather to achieve any real change for the future economic prospects of the millennials, that they intuitively knew that they would have to create disruptive (more inclusive) corporations for themselves which would have to compete head on with the self-serving corporations of old, by connecting immediately to the general public directly. To Robert, it's like the transformation that has taken place in the environmental movement, where not so long ago environmentally oblivious corporations might care less as to their environmental image because they thought themselves to be impervious to the environmental cause; as opposed to today's culture where each corporation is now trying to outdo each other in demonstrating just how environmentally friendly each corporation can be. Similarly, the millennials could potentially create a counter culture revolution within the corporate market place where only those corporations that are aspiring to alleviate mass inequality, wage disparity, unemployment and oppression, are to win the lion's share of any particular industrial market share. Leaving those that don't assume such a mantra, to be stigmatized as being the dinosaurs of greed and corruption that once injured so many for so long, and brought the American economy on so many occasions to its very knees.

So for Robert, underneath Maddi's and Patrick's proposal (similar to those other ideas that stem from the shared economy perspective) was a progressive initiative that would allow the better part of America (the good and less selfish traits of the majority of the American people) to bypass the system of old, by using a corporate model for fundamental change to build new corporate agendas, where profits (although still of primary importance) would only be but one aspect amongst others (like the environment, being equally important) working for the benefit of the people by making some of the better homes in New York City accessible to the middle class. These are the ideas, which are revolutionary, and their strength would still be financially strong as the silent American majority through its collective presence makes its wishes known in each industry, through its command over market share.

And although a skeptic might assume that only profit centered corporations are to prosper in today's globally competitive world, the events since 08 would suggest that since so much of the worlds wealth can be lost or put at risk due to fraud and corruption while government and private agencies (that were specifically created to prevent such things from happening) standby while crimes are being committed; then it is likely that there will be a large future market for blue chip corporations with identifiable assets, that are cleaner than the rest, that will be in high demand in the near and distant future. And what Maddi probably didn't understand was that the actual strength of her initiative rested not only with the product she was proposing but was equally strong because of its simple attempt to be up front and honest. Put simply, middle class Americans would accept less appreciation in future property value in exchange for the ability to live better and more financially secure in the here and now. Her corporation would be a disruptive force simply because it was that simple, that unselfish, and most of all, that honest. And as far as pension plans were concerned, the prospect of investing themselves as a corporate structure into something so tangible and straightforward, such as investing in the long term value of Manhattan real estate, would probably also have its appeal to those who are more risk adverse. Basically, Maddi's corporate plan would be to have regular Americans invest their future with other regular Americans who would then jointly own their future together. And in a world where the corruption of the elite has cost regular Americans so much, Robert saw Maddi's plan as a pretty safe bet. So, just as there were good Americans in the south that had always opposed slavery, and just as there were suffragettes before there were suffragettes, the question now is: are there those within corporate America today with the vision enough to make America, or Great Britain or France, or Germany the next moral (and economic) superpower, by simply recognizing that the most honest corporate state is in the 21st century, is also to be the most reliable and the most desirable and stable place to live, and to invest, and to do business, ... in a world that otherwise, is corruptly going to hell.

Consequently, regardless of whichever nation that this moral economic high ground happens, it will be the millennial force that makes it happen. Especially now, by virtue of the fact that through the advent of social media, the world has benefitted from the fact that the elite of the world no longer control the message, or at least not all of it; therefore, the corporate message of the future is the millennials to command. One of Robert's students in seizing upon this lesson in one of Robert's business classes, in a term paper tried to demonstrate that the message of reform could be commandeered by creating and separating young millennials from the hypocritical and fraudulent ways of the past by creating or perfecting a brand for corporate consciousness by creating advantageous slogans that could be copyrighted or trademarked that would in effect turn the tables on the "us vs. them" paradigm. As an example, one slogan (that the student knew the Professor would personally like) was a sticker slogan that could be sold to future entrepreneurs that would create a moral bond of social consciousness (much like the famed slogan: "Made in America") that read: "I am an honest millennial, are you?" Needless to say, Robert was being played, but he knew he was being well played, and for all the right reasons ... so that paper got an "A." But so as to humble the student somewhat, Robert then wrote in the margin that (provided that no child labor or sweat shops were used) he would have given him an "A+" if the student had actually sold the idea to the Swedish clothing giant H&M, suggesting that they adopt the side slogan that: "Hennes & Mauritz are also, Honest & Millennial".

In making this point near the end of the academic year, Robert would try to tie his message together by demonstrating that so pervasive is the fraudulent activity in both politics and business today that even those who are supposed to help protect us from such things, are themselves too frequently engaged in some form of fraud or betrayal of their own; and in global breadth, this goes well beyond the type of neglect that the bond rating agencies engaged in during the crisis of 08. The simple truth, is that these frauds and betrayals are everywhere. In fact, so pervasive and far reaching are these betrayals and failures, that they are routinely being chronicled in the mass media, because as in 'a death by a thousand cuts,' we have now become so systematically desensitized as to the systemic failures of all that we have been promised that it is unclear now if the perpetrators even care about whether or not they get caught. For example, the credit monitoring agency Equifax, one of the dominant credit score agencies within the United States was showcased on 60 Minutes in 2013 demonstrating that not only do many of its staff work outside the US but that of the millions of complaints that Equifax receives every year, as to inaccurate reports on individual American credit scores; when a complaint is made demonstrating that there has been a terrible mistake in reporting some one's credit score, that where there is supposed to be an investigation to set matters straight, the truth is that there is little or no investigation at all.

So for Robert when he is trying to inspire his students as the term comes to an end, and Robert realizes that he may never see some of these students again, and yet he wants to instill in them a sense of hope for the future; he attempts to show them that although the task of succeeding against the established rich appears at present daunting, he reminds them that sometimes that particularly unique solutions can be found when you actually tackle two problems at once. Reminding the students that the decay of the world right now is premised on a determination by the wealthy to increase the disparity gap in wealth (through hoarding) and by doing so (hoarding currency reserves and by doing big business only amongst themselves) that they have created (quite deliberately) a liquidity shortage (for larger loans) to the majority of property-less citizens. This is one problem. A second problem is that the dishonesty that is readily apparent at the top of the financial 'food chain' is also doing little to dissuade average Americans and the rest of the world's masses, that they should not follow our leader's example, because by adopting (the tricks of the casino) out in the real world, by rigging the world's economy against the interests of each nation's citizenry, such actions in the public domain no longer carry with them the exemption of being voluntary. Rather when casino tactics are used in public affairs, they carry with them the stench of deceit and betrayal, the same sort of dishonesty and hypocrisy that was used to implement the likes of slavery during cruder times, because cloaked in finance, in these more sophisticated times; such exploitative tendencies (when there is no place else for the people to go) becomes the destructive immorality of our time. Robert's closing message is that the 21st century, is in a very real sense, the discovery of a "new world" all over again; where the millennials can choose a different course, distinct and different than the corruption, betrayal, or hypocrisy of our ancestors. Of course it is common knowledge, Robert points out, that Thomas Jefferson in treatment of his slaves during his lifetime that he (who was the chief architect of the Declaration of Independence) refused to even follow George Washington's gesture of freeing his slaves upon his death. Similarly, because the millennials find the "old world" in the way that it is; in the "new world" of instantaneous direct communication, the millennials have a choice as a consumer force, to once again choose the type of people they wish to be. Consequently, America, (or any other western nation for that matter) can again now choose a different course than that of the past. The millennials through worldwide communication (and buying power) can turn the tables on the ancient paradigm of "us vs. them" where in this "new world millennium" the good can stake out their own corporate agenda and through consolidation and mass buying power can put the corrupt (by declaring them to be so) back on their heels, and they will be able to do this through their sheer command over any particular industry's market share.

To make his point and to bring his suggestion down to earth, Robert's points to the catastrophic failure by our national authorities to provide the necessary oversight in matters of extreme trust such as in the case of the Equifax failures, Robert has put to his students the possibility of seizing an opportunity and creating a new solution by proposing an alternate corporate choice for people to go to in determining the credit worthiness of any given individual. The potential solution to the societal failures (such as those which have occurred with Equifax) would be for the millennials to create an alternate list, a parallel list (at least for the immediate future) whereby people in need of credit and a credit history could go to an on line institution where they could get both, Robert likes to call this solution, the "Reputation Bank." A Reputation Bank could be an institutional alternative to Equifax that could serve as both a place where one could obtain a loan and an immediate credit reference when needed. A Reputation Bank would be something like where an Angie's List partners up with a Payday Loans or a Quicken Loans facility. The purpose would be to fix two problems with one solution. The idea would be that a number of private investors could loan their own funds or underwrite the advancement of loans to less affluent individuals at some negotiated repayment schedule, and the status of the loan would be readily available for inspection by the entire public through access to the internet. This would allow individuals who are without a credit history, or who are in need of either: readily available credit, or a credit reference, could get such a loan solely on the basis of the strength of one's own reputation. Such a "Reputation Bank" would operate on the strength of one's word and it would therefore be like an honesty and dependability catalogue that could be made readily access able to the public for viewing through the internet using as collateral, those who just always keep their word. Naturally, of course in exchange for this sort of trust, the borrowers would have to forgo the usual sense of privacy that is offered with the more usual collateralized loans that come from our more typical banks; but it would be a reliable and immediate safety net for those whom our most wealthy would simply just turn away. Hilary Clinton has recently suggested that: too many (American) dreams die in the parking lots of banks. Well here is a viable solution to such a problem. Of course, any failure to repay the loan would also be available for all to see, but that's the whole point; the purpose of such an institution would be (at least in part) to put a premium on a person's word and a hand shake, so as to allow the less affluent an opportunity to have ready access to liquidity, and to build up a strong and reliable credit score, producing both at the same time. But possibly more important than these two advantages; as a nation, we would be reestablishing our core American values held by the majority towards fairness, honesty and integrity, as being the very foundation for one's rightful ascent to prosperity; as opposed to the current reality where apparently fraud, deception and betrayal seem to accomplish the same.

The intangible benefits of such an alternative mechanism could be immense on so many levels. First with an emphasis on promises made and promises kept; such an institutional backing of such core values would help to build a bridge between the non-political/ backbone of America and the already existing moneyed establishment within America. While it could also build a bridge (depending on how the loans were structured) between "the haves" and "the have nots" as a direct connection could be made between the lender and the borrower as a more collaborative, trusting, long lasting, productive financial relationships could be forged to the benefit of all. This was part of what Martin Luther King was possibly referring to in his famous "I Have a Dream" speech where he envisioned a nation where all would be judged "by the content of their character." A nationally endorsed Reputation Bank could be a meaningful step in that regard, while also countermanding by example (and by putting on display) all those who would choose more destructive and regressive selfish pursuits.

These are the challenges and the possibilities, facing today's millennials, both young and old. And although some may foolishly believe that since they currently have a job, that these concerns are not theirs to tackle, but by accepting things the way they are for now; the lessons of 08 tell us that by allowing those in control to use what they know about us, not for us but against us; means that we stay forever expendable and disposable to them. Staying complacent while times appear to be good is like staying at the casino tables while you are still ahead. The time to change (or renegotiate) the odds in a game that we can no longer walk away from, is now; before the next crisis. Also, blindly allowing our current drone status to become methodically the oppression of our time is not freedom. Today's complacent drone, who fails to see that things are becoming increasingly tight, is tomorrows unemployed. Waiting for the next collapse, denying the fact that most of us live in the fear that we (subconsciously) know we are but one step away from true poverty, ... such is not living, and it is certainly not ... the pursuit of happiness. The time for us to renegotiate and to revamp our institutions, is now. And with this cautionary warning, Robert (each semester) ends his final class with: "Now Let the Real (and the Honest) American Revolution, Begin!" Now, if Robert could only just help Patrick and Maddi find the necessary multi-million dollar financing... for their shared housing project, that they need! ... C'mon America!

www.ingramcontent.com/pod-product-compliance
Lightning Source LLC
Chambersburg PA
CBHW070809290326
41931CB00011BB/2174